I0812046

Constructivism

Translation and introduction by Christina Lodder

Aleksei Gan

TENOV

First published in December 2013

© of the translation and introduction: Christina Lodder

© of V. Stepanova's illustrations and A. Rodchenko's pictures: The A. Rodchenko & V. Stepanova Archive, Moscow.

The author and publishers should like to take this opportunity to express their enormous gratitude to the Lavrentiev family and particularly to Alexander Lavrentiev, who has been extremely helpful in answering all our queries and exceedingly generous in allowing us to reproduce the wonderful photographs made by his grandfather, Alexander Rodchenko.

© of this edition:
Editorial Tenov
Casp 147
08013 Barcelona
tenov@editorialtenov.com
www.tenovbooks.com

ALL POSSIBLE EFFORTS HAVE BEEN MADE TO CONTACT COPYRIGHT HOLDERS. Any omission or error is regretted and should be notified to the publisher.

All rights reserved. This publication may not be reproduced, stored in a retrieval system or transmitted in any form or by any means, electronic, mechanical, photocopying, recording or otherwise, without prior permission of the publishers.

Printed with PJS & C impressions, Barcelona.

ISBN: 978-84-939231-2-9
DL: B 29511-2013

Published with the support of the Institute for Literary Translation, Russia.

ИНСТИТУТ ПЕРЕВОДА

AD VERBUM

CONTENTS

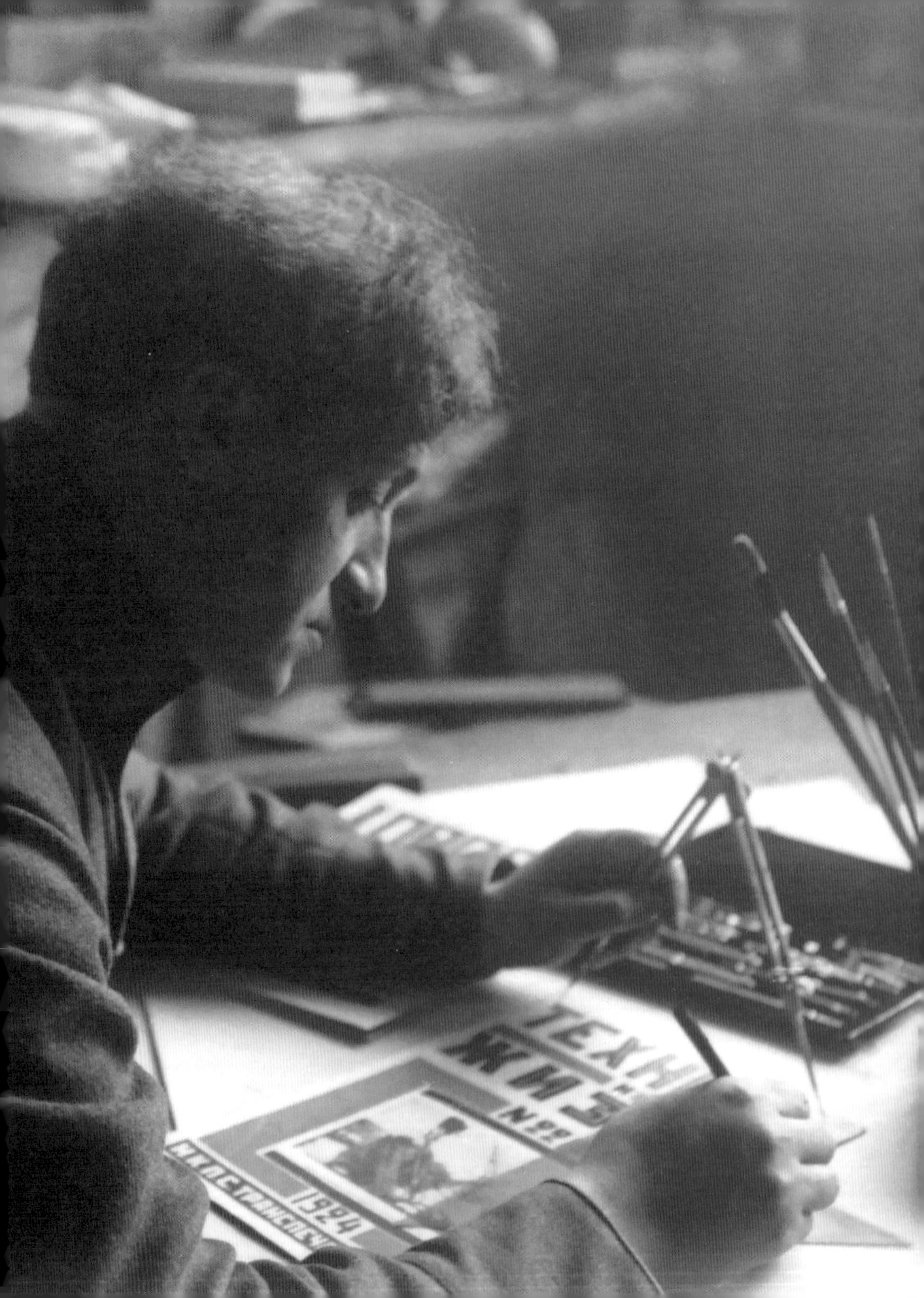
1924

ALEKSEI GAN: A PIVOTAL FIGURE IN RUSSIAN CONSTRUCTIVISM

Christina Lodder

Constructivism was a revolutionary creative movement in Russia in the 1920s and Aleksei Mikhailovich Gan was a crucial figure in its development. Yet, until the 1990s, very little had been written about him.[1] Ironically, the first articles devoted exclusively to him appeared during that decade, which also saw the collapse of the Soviet Union and the final destruction of any hopes concerning the creation of a communist utopia in Russia, of which he had dreamed and for which he had worked so assiduously.[2] Unfortunately, although the fall of communism meant that archive materials now became available, Russian rejection of the Revolution and the dominance of Western postmodernism at the time meant that the intellectual appeal of figures like Gan plummeted. Since then, however, scholarly interest has revived in both Russia and the West. Alexander Lavrentiev has published his valuable monograph on this enigmatic cultural figure,[3] while Kristin Romberg has shed new light on his life and work.[4] In writing this introduction I have benefitted enormously from their research.

The name of Aleksei Gan has not always played a very large role in histories of Russian Constructivism, although he actually made a vital contribution to the formulation, elaboration, publication and promotion of Constructivist theory and practice. He was the author of the Programme of the Moscow-based Working Group of Constructivists in March 1921; he published the first theoretical treatise about the movement, *Constructivism* (*Konstruktivizm* of October-December 1922); and was responsible for editing two important journals, which elaborated Constructivist theory and developed Constructivist practice in relation to film, photography and architecture: *Cinema-Photo* (*Kino-Fot*, 1922-1923), and *Contemporary Architecture* (*Sovremennaya arkhitektura – SA*, 1926-1930). These journals published relevant texts by figures working in these fields, explained and promoted Constructivism in general, and fostered related ideas. In addition to his promotional and theoretical work, Gan also designed some of the first kiosks embodying Constructivist principles, developed the theory and practice of typography along Constructivist lines, and worked in theatre and film.

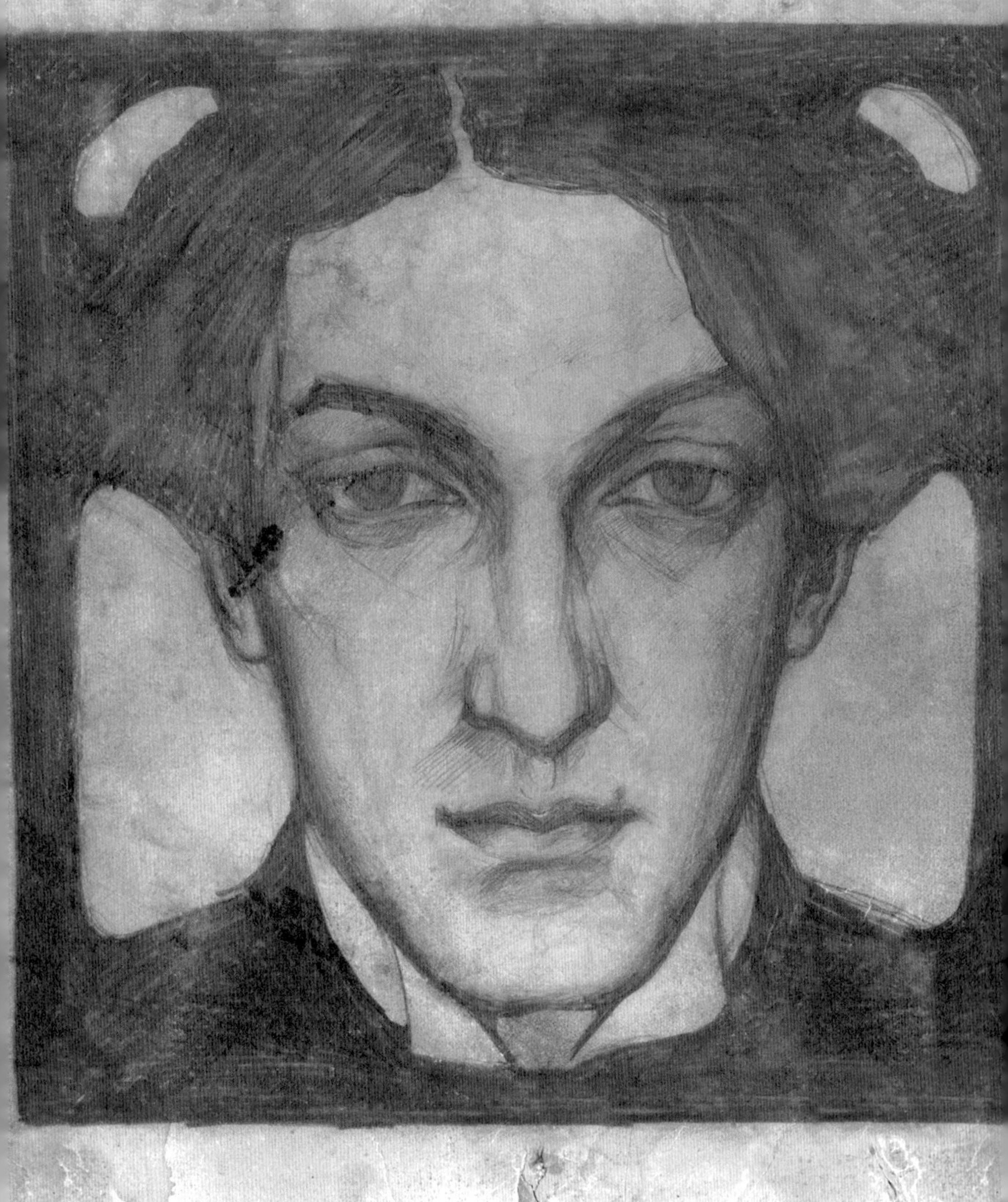

This list of varied activities suggests one of the reasons why Gan has been treated rather cursorily by art historians writing about Constructivism – he is difficult to categorise. He was a cultural and political activist, an eclectic and talented figure, who had a finger in a whole range of avant-garde pies, but was not pre-eminent in any of them. In many respects, the variety and range of his activities reflect the way in which Constructivism itself was an inter-disciplinary movement, embracing a large number of different media.

Naturally, art historians writing about Constructivism have tended to focus on the group of artists who moved from making works of art to devising objects for everyday use, and, although Gan produced a few designs, he was not a prolific designer nor was he directly involved in developing a Constructivist design methodology at the Moscow Vkhutemas (*Vysshie khudozhestvenno-tekhnicheskie masterskie* – Higher Artistic and Technical Workshops), where Aleksandr Rodchenko, Lyubov Popova, Varvara Stepanova, Aleksandr Vesnin, Gustavs Klucis (Gustav Klutsis) and others worked on the Basic Course and in the Wood and Metal Working faculties.[5] Equally significant for his posthumous reputation, Gan was not involved – and not even mentioned – in the prominent avant-garde journal *Lef: Left Front of the Arts* (*Levyi front iskusstv*, 1923-1925), edited by the poet Vladimir Mayakovsky. *Lef* was primarily concerned with literature, but it did contain several significant articles and theoretical statements about Constructivism, as well as illustrating several works by Rodchenko, Stepanova and Popova. Gan produced some important designs for kiosks, but neither these nor his typographical works are as well-known as those of Rodchenko or Klucis. Even as the theorist of the movement, Gan was more of an agitator, publisher, activist and promoter than a subtle aesthetician. Significantly, Stepanova observed in March 1920, "Gan considers that agitation is just as important as creating works of art".[6]

To compound such disadvantages, information about Gan's life and career has been tantalising scarce. For many years, we did not even know the exact dates of his birth or death. It now appears that he was born in 1887, officially arrested in 1941 and shot in 1942.[7] In 1934, having been commissioned by a publisher to do some work in the Far East of the Soviet Union, he went to Khabarovsk.[8] There, he decorated the port for the return of the crew of the S. S. Chelyuskin, which had sunk in 1934, while exploring the North Maritime Route through the Arctic. Subsequently, Gan seems to have disappeared, although at some point he swore at Stalin in public, calling him "a pock-marked swine" (*ryaboi svoloch'*) – an act that was undoubtedly linked to his incarceration and death.[9] He was rehabilitated in 1989.[10]

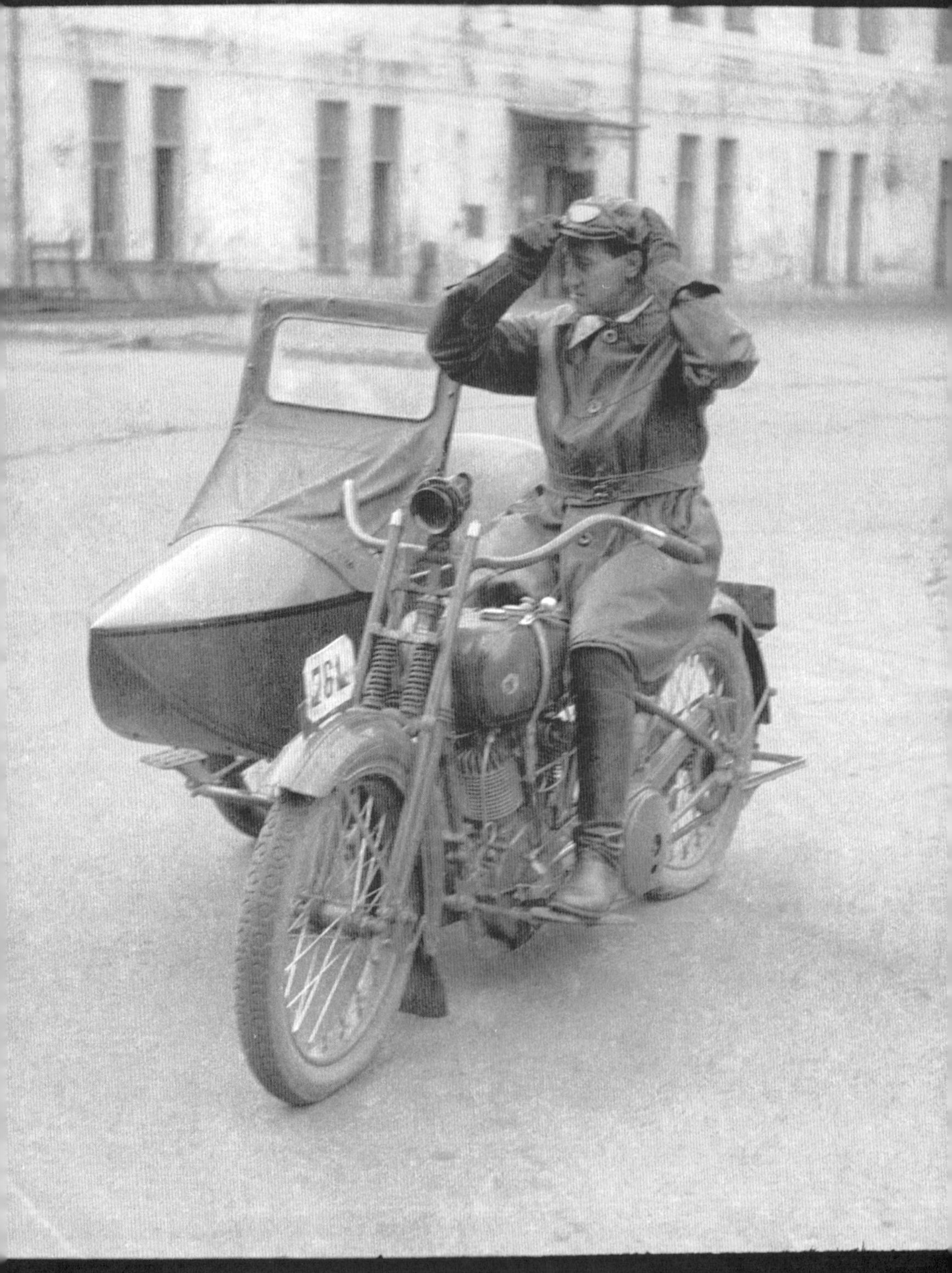
26L

Even today, Gan's education and personal life before the Revolution are shrouded in a certain degree of mystery. His first wife, Olga, died in February 1920 from some kind of heart disease.[11] His second wife was the film-maker Esfir Shub, whom he met while working in the Theatrical Department of the Commissariat for Enlightenment (*Teatral'noe otdelenie, Narodnyi komissariat prosveshcheniya* – TEO, Narkompros).[12] Anna Konopleva, his step-daughter, recalls that he was active in the political underground, had a pleasant tenor voice, once sung in an opera, fought in the First World War, liked baking, kept his studio extremely clean and tidy, was a kind man, but was also an alcoholic and periodically went on drunken binges.[13] His alcoholism seems to have been responsible for his extended stays in hospital. In the mid-1920s, he was a patient at the Z. P. Solovev Moscow Municipal Psychiatric Hospital No. 8, and in November 1928 was admitted to the Donskoi psychiatric hospital.[14] Alcoholism may also have prevented him attaining his full potential, as is inferred by his colleague, the Constructivist architect Viktor Vesnin:

> A man of exceptionally profound and wide-ranging talents, A. M. Gan played a very important and leading role in Soviet graphics, cinema and architecture. Extremely well educated and with an outstanding knowledge of Marxist-Leninist literature, Gan aspired to fulfil the great social task of our times in all his artistic work. Unfortunately, Gan's illness almost always prevented him realising the best of his artistic ideas and so his potential powers were never fully realised.[15]

Gan is chiefly remembered for his connection with Constructivism, but, as far as we know, he did not receive any artistic training and there is no evidence that he worked as a professional artist before the Revolution, although he was undoubtedly interested in art since a self-portrait from the 1910s has survived (p. X). His avant-garde colleagues clearly did not regard him as an artist. In early 1919, Stepanova reported Rodchenko saying "I am sick to death of Gan. He understands nothing about art".[16] In contrast to his artistic friends, however, Gan evidently had more than a superficial knowledge of science and technology. He rode a motorcycle and was able to repair it, and on 28 August 1921, he was elected president of the Association of Inventors (*Assotsiatsiia izobretatelei* – AIZ).[17] It is not clear what he invented, but he was evidently valued as someone with scientific and technological skills.

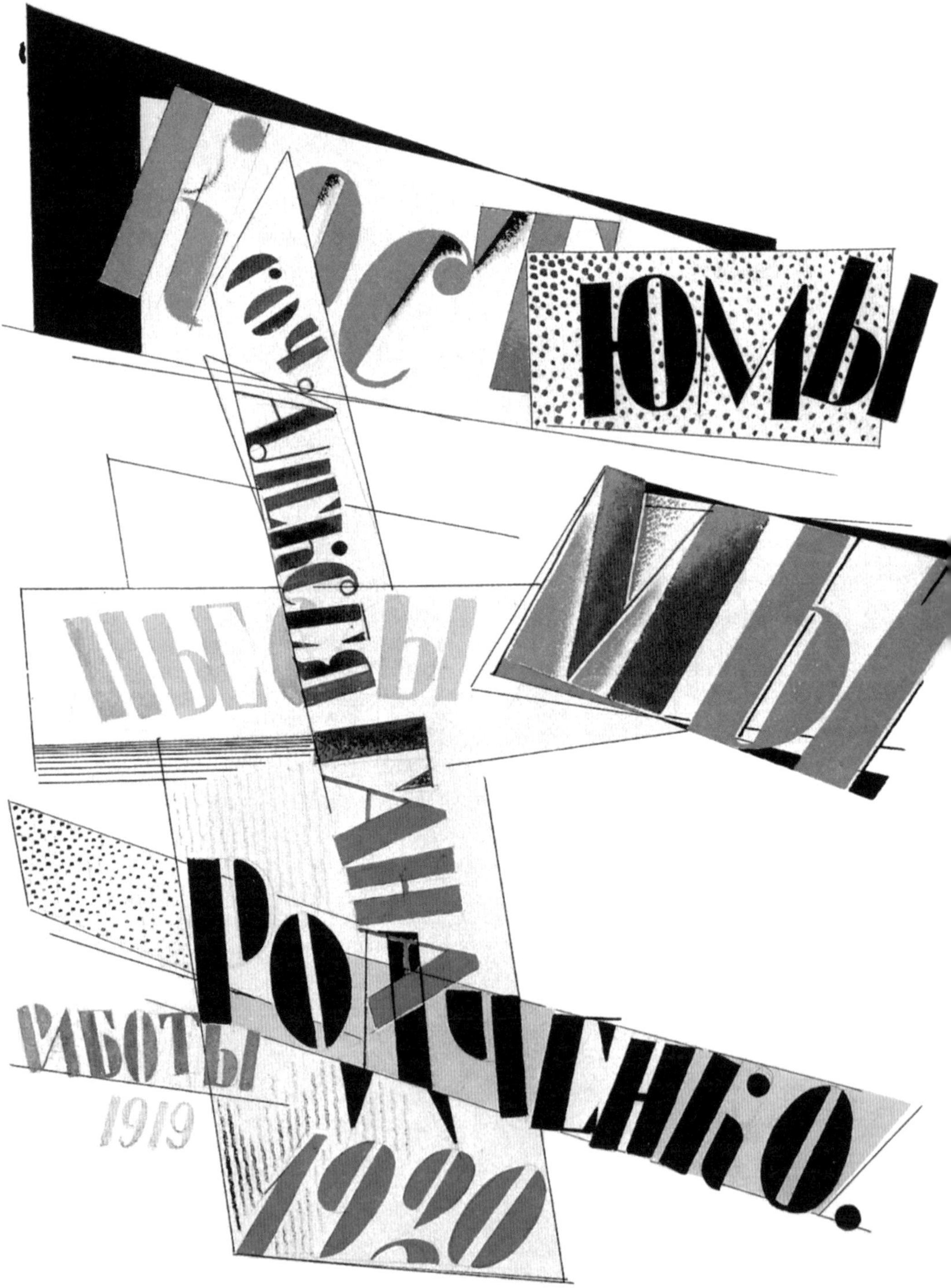
КОСТЮМЫ
СОЧ. АЛЕКСЕЯ ГАНА
ПЬЕСЫ
МЫ
РАБОТЫ
РОДЧЕНКО
1919
1920

Revolutionary Theatre

Initially, Gan's sphere of cultural expertise seems to have been the theatre rather than art. Apparently he had been involved with workers' amateur dramatics before the Revolution,[18] and between the February and October Revolutions of 1917, organised an amateur dramatics group for the Moscow Union of Food Workers, placing it under the patronage of the Moscow Federation of Anarchist Groups in 1918.[19] Gan argued that the workers themselves should create the new theatre, and stressed, "contemporary proletarian theatre – is not art. It is vital creative work. It neither understands nor accepts an alien repertoire. It is creating its own repertoire".[20] A history of the Russian theatre published in 1933, described Gan as "the ideologist of decadent abstraction",[21] who had embraced the ideas of Proletkult (the organisation dedicated to fostering proletarian culture, set up in 1918 by Aleksandr Bogdanov, Maxim Gorky and Anatolii Lunacharskii),[22] and had manipulated the theatrical section of the Soviet of Worker and Peasant Theatre to declare its intention "to fight without compromise against the professional Theatres".[23] Proletkult had lost its independence in 1921, and Gan was clearly out of favour by the 1930s, but the Proletkult connection is probably valid, since his standpoint reflected Proletkult policy and he cited Bogdanov quite extensively in his *Constructivism* text of 1922. In early 1919, Gan joined TEO, and in 1920, he set up the group of "Mass Action" (*Massovoe deistvie*) with Vitalii Zhemchuzhnyi and N. Lvov.[24] Reiterating Gan's previous statements, this body asserted "The question of the creation of mass theatre can only be solved by the masses themselves in the process of collective creative work and comradely co-operation between the leadership and the collectives."[25]

Gan's opposition to the professional theatre changed when he saw Vsevolod Meyerkhold's production of the Belgian symbolist poet Émile Verhaeren's play *The Dawn* of 1915. In this, the revolutionaries within two warring armies unite against the tyranny of the generals and capitalists, declaring peace and celebrating the international solidarity of the working class. Meyerhold's production had evoked the revolutionary spirit of the times by presenting the play "in the style of a political rally", while the auditorium's interior was so informal that "everyone felt like the master in this theatre".[26] Reviewing the play in November 1920, Gan wrote:

> The fight that I have been waging until now against the professional theatre in general, must now be changed somewhat, since the appearance of the new theatre of the RSFSR embodies a substantial adjustment in its

> conception of the theatre as a sacred temple. It seems that it is possible to leave this temple, talk with the actors, fire them with revolutionary enthusiasm and fight within the theatre itself for a path towards the new audience. We must now direct all our efforts towards educating and organising that audience.[27]

It seems to have been around 1920, during the period of crisis concerning the new repertoire, that Gan wrote his play *We* (p. XIV). The text hasn't survived – just a list of characters and Rodchenko's colourful costume designs, which Gan had asked the artist to create on 29 November 1920.[28] Rodchenko recorded, "in all, thirty sketches for the revolutionary dynamic play *We* by Aleksei Gan. I proposed making the costumes myself according to a new principle."[29] The workers' costumes were to be "made of only red tones (red on red) and based on textural contrasts", while the policeman was to be produced in the same way, only using black tones (pp. XVIII-XIX).[30] The surviving designs indicate that, as in Vladimir Mayakovsky's play, *Mystery Bouffe* (1918), Gan had divided his characters into the "clean" (the worker, peasant and clown – i.e. those to whom the revolutionary future belongs) and the "unclean" (the officer and the merchant – the capitalists and bourgeoisie representing the oppressors of the past). Since no script has ever been located, Alexander Lavrentiev has suggested that Gan conceived the play as a mass spectacle with the audience participating fully in creating the action of the play.[31]

This is possible, since Gan was a great advocate of Mass Theatre when he worked for the Section for Mass Performances and Spectacles within TEO, and this is mentioned in a report of 5-8 February 1920. Acknowledging that the first of May was "an integral festival of proletarian culture", and that "the scenario should be written by the masses themselves in the process of collective work and collective discussion", the section adopted Gan's suggestion that the celebrations should be based on the Communist International, "from which the international festival historically emerges, as the first act of mass creativity on a world scale".[32] It would therefore be about the history of the three communist internationals, culminating in "a vivid portrayal of the great achievements of the October Revolution, the Soviet system and of the transition to socialist forms of life." The report added:

> A. M. Gan has elaborated in detail the decorative side of the festivities, the layout of the "stage" on which the festivities are to unfold, and which will ultimately expand to encompass not only the entire city of Moscow, but even its outskirts.

> The overall aim of this plan is to imagine the communist city of the future. All the squares on which the action is to take place will be named after the arts and sciences. For example, Geography Square – with a huge globe on which the continents are painted in the red shade of a flaming world revolution – Astronomy Square, Political Economy Square, etc.
> The streets will be decorated with red flags and shop windows with satirical depictions of themes of a topical nature. Somewhere out of town (possibly at Khodynka) a field of the International will be set up with a radio station and an aerodrome. The main action of the festivities will be played out on this field.
> The part of the festival scenario elaborated in most detail by the Section is the prologue, which is outlined in the following form. Early in the morning a loud siren will sound on the Sparrow Hills, which will be answered by the horns of all the city's factories.
> At this signal, cavalry patrols, motor-cycles and vehicles will leave the seventeen outposts of Moscow for the district squares, summoning the citizens into the streets. On the district squares, they will be awaited by agitation collectives who will draw the people into active participation in the festival. Here the act of the first international will be performed.
> On its completion, the masses will start moving towards the centre, passing along the streets and squares of the arts and sciences. The celebration of the Second International will be held in the centre.
> Finally, the crowds of people will move towards the Field of the International where the collapse of the Second International will be enacted, followed by the emergence of the Third, and the transition to a socialist system. Along the way, intervals for food and rest will be arranged, which will also take the form of theatre.[33]

Gan's plans were not executed. In fact, a report of the actual May Day festivities in Moscow described posters and decorations, that culminated in a performance of Sophocles' play *Oedipus*.[34] In search of "proletarian purity", Gan had rejected such classical components as well as the example of the French Revolution's festivities as "the deposits of alien cults".[35] Nevertheless, there is clearly a connection between Gan's scheme and the *Project for a Theatrical Military Parade for the Congress of The Third International: The End of Capital*, which his colleagues Aleksandr Vesnin, Popova and Meyerkhold planned to enact the following year on the Khodyn Field in Moscow.[36] Sadly, this also was not realised.[37]

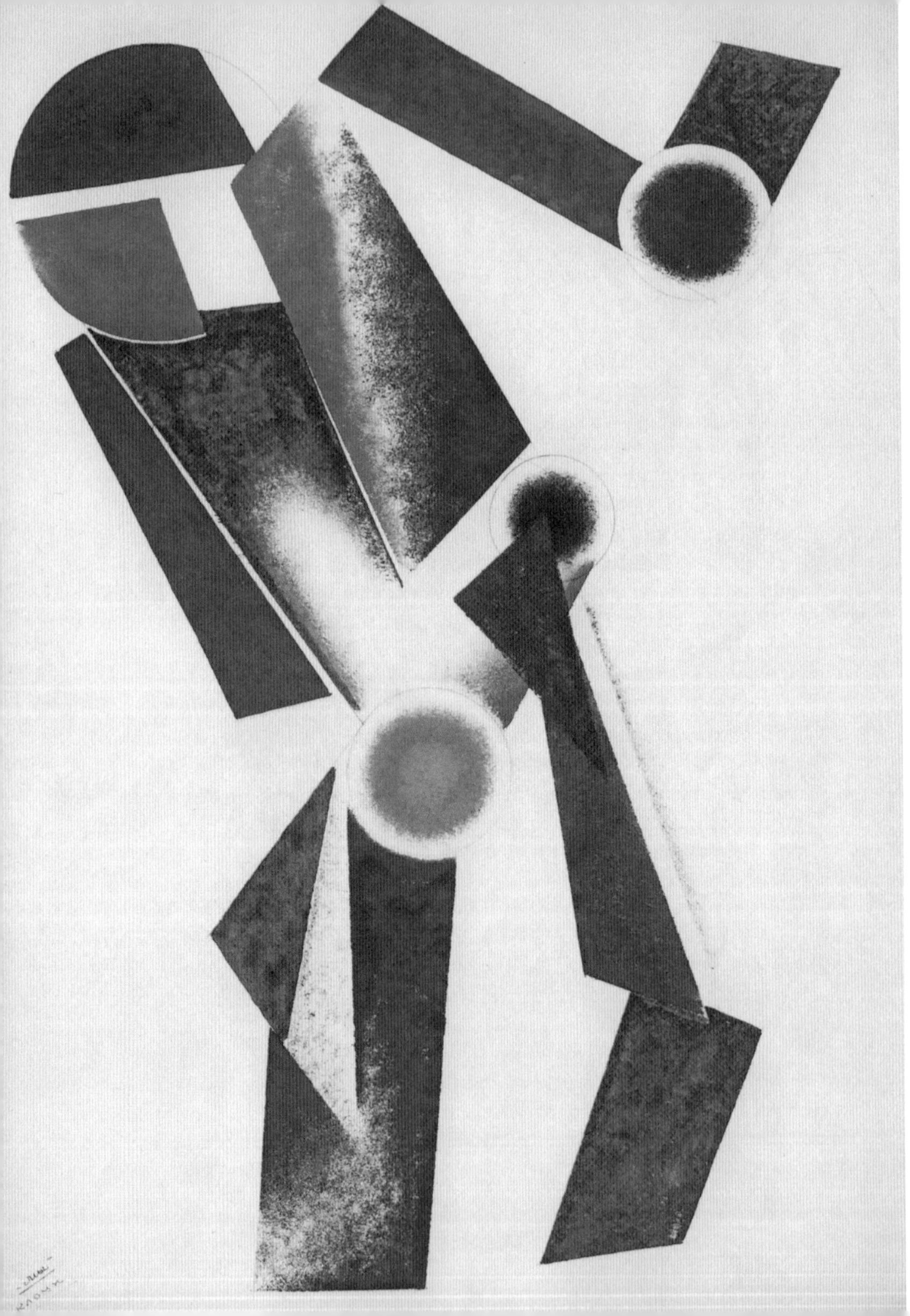
КЛОУН

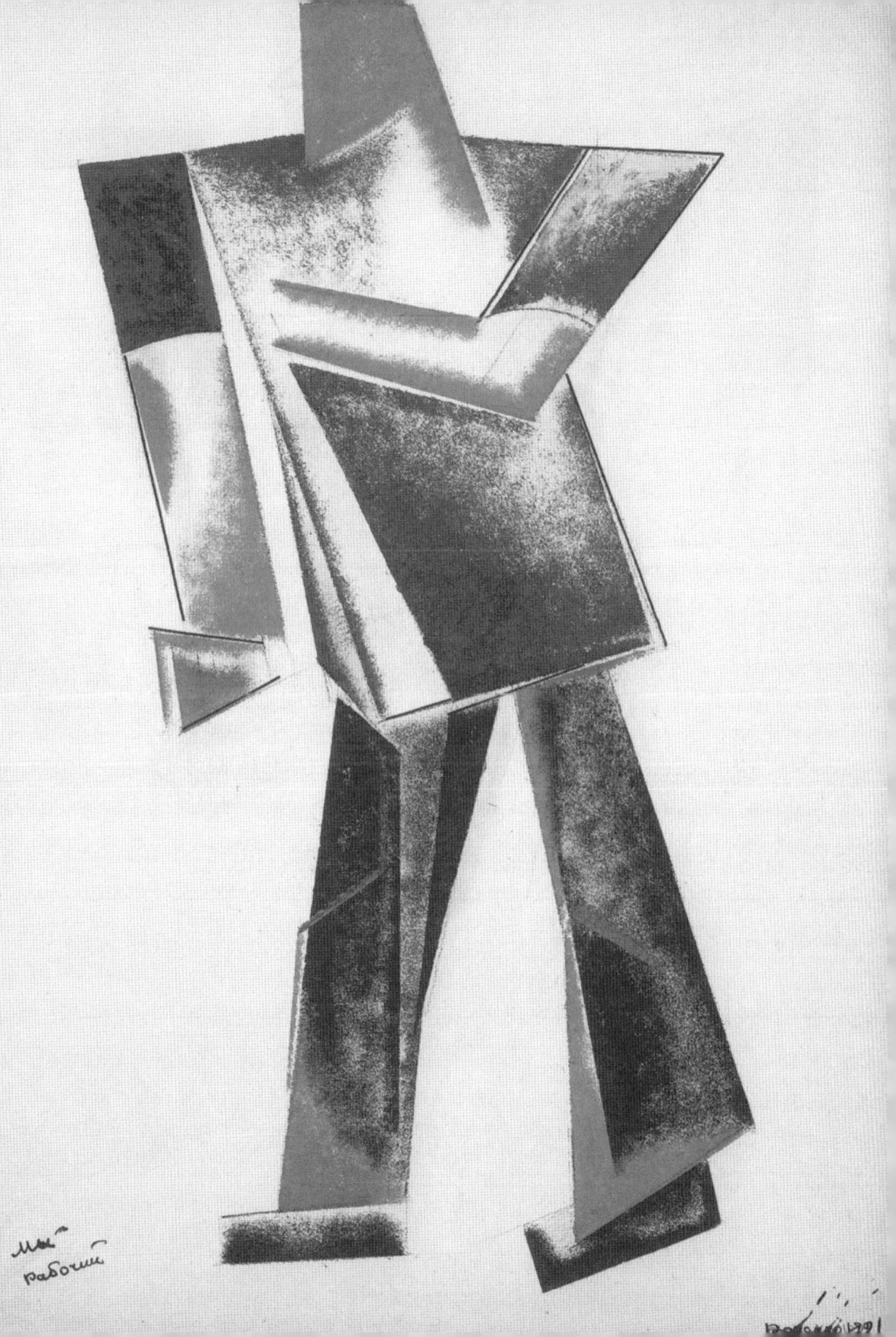
Мой
рабочий

Forging Links with Avant-Garde Artists

Gan seems to have established his first contacts with the artistic avant-garde in early 1918, when the Moscow Soviet of Workers', Peasants and Red Army Deputies (*Moskovskii sovet rabochikh krest'yanskikh i krasnoarmeiskikh deputatov*) made him responsible for the important art collections of Sergei Shchukin and Ivan Morozov.[38] It was apparently in this connection, in early 1918, that he first met the artists Vladimir Tatlin, Aleksei Morgunov and Rodchenko. The latter recalled:

> Tatlin and Morgunov, having received credentials from the Moscow Soviet of Worker and Peasant Deputies to negotiate the guarding of private townhouses from looting, to follow up on it went to see Gan. They took me along to the meeting. That's where I met Aleksei Gan.[39]

At this time, Gan was also working for the short-lived anarchist newspaper *Anarchy* (*Anarkhiya*, published by the Moscow Federation of Anarchist Groups – *Moskovskaya federatsiya anarkhicheskikh grupp)* as editor of the "Art" (*Iskusstvo*) section, later called "Creative Work" (*Tvorchestvo*).[40] His first contribution to the newspaper ("The Revolution and the People's Theatre") had appeared in number 12.[41] Under his guidance, the art section, which was introduced in number 15, became a forum for the avant-garde and a valuable mouthpiece for their ideas.[42] It was there that Tatlin, Kazimir Malevich, Rodchenko, Ivan Klyun and others published texts about art and the Revolution. The "Creative Work" section thus contains some of the earliest (and most revealing) artists' statements concerning their evolving attitudes towards the social and political changes occurring in Russia. On 23 March 1918, Malevich, Morgunov, and Gan published "The Problem of Art and the Role of its Suppressors", which attacked the "poison of bourgeois banality" and the "high priests of bourgeois taste", who were now attempting to re-exert their influence on art, just when "democracy is creating a proletarian culture".[43] At this time, Gan was also agitating for the creation of a House of Contemporary Art (*Dom sovremennogo iskusstva*) on the basis of the nationalised collections of Shchukin and Morozov.[44]

Subsequently, the newspaper decided to publish a separate collection of essays by Gan, Malevich, Rodchenko, and others, under the title *Anarchy-Creative Work* (*Anarkhiya-Tvórchestvo*). An announcement, on 30 May 1918, described its contents and the thinking behind its conception:

> Our newspaper cannot afford to offer more space to the problems of art and creative work. We have decided to publish a collection [of articles] dealing exclusively with the problems concerning the destructive and creative innovation of today in our construction of culture. The book is divided into three parts:
> The first part will deal with agitation; part two with dynamite and form; part three with information ... going over the heads of dealers, critics and the whole gang of obliging philanthropists ... we have decided, like destructive dynamite, to rise and fall with our forms of creative innovation into the very thick of the masses.[45]

During the early revolutionary period, the anarchists supported the Bolsheviks, and so Gan, like many creative and intellectual figures, whose primary loyalty seems to have been to anarchism at this point, did not seem to experience any problem in combining allegiances. It was, however, an uneasy alliance, and on 12 April 1918, the Bolsheviks attacked 26 anarchist centres in Moscow. At this point, Gan seems to have remained within the anarchist camp, as a public speech given on 7 June 1918 indicates:

> At the end of this month, the first collection "Anarchy-Creative Work" will be published. In addition, we have decided to participate more in meetings with workers and share with them our ideas about creating a new anarchist-proletarian art and culture ...
> Recently, we have been receiving a lot of requests from comrade workers, who themselves want to take part in this process. They are turning to the anarchists, because they understand a major aspect of our work; we do not impose any dogmas, neither do we confine or restrict the individual's creative potential; instead we broaden his horizons *ad infinitum* ...
> Seven years ago, our Futurists had already presented a "slap in the face of public taste".[46] These defiant souls began a great rebellion against the bourgeois order in art, against the old rationality of arrogant bourgeois rule. The old generals of art had good reason to meet them with indignation. But why are the gentlemen "Marxists" and other "Socialists" now screaming so loudly against the Futurists and other rebellious innovators?
> Is there not hypocrisy hidden behind their screams?
> Yes it is hidden.
> That is why we, anarchist artists, are bravely penetrating this wretched, many-headed monster of former educators and, together with the

Futurists and Suprematists, are destroying these new prisons of rotten ideas in the Sections of their Jesuitical Education.
We are pitting our contemporary creative work against the old art.[47]

While Gan was still clearly loyal to anarchism in the summer of 1918, using a vocabulary resonant with concepts of individual liberty and the destruction of tradition, by January 1919, he was less partisan, announcing, "I work with anarchists, maximalists and Bolsheviks".[48] Indeed, he may have joined the Bolshevik Party towards the end of 1918.[49] Certainly, by spring 1919, he was working for the Red Army, specifically for the Moscow District Commissariat for Military Affairs as Head of the Cultural Education Department, responsible for conducting "cultural education and an all-sided education of the troops in the spirit of the idea of communism"[50]. Apparently, he gave his lectures and talks in a variety of buildings (such as clubs, theatres, libraries) and "within the military units themselves", liaising with local Communist Party organisations and Narkompros.[51] Not surprisingly, by the time that anarchism was finally suppressed in 1921, at the end of the Civil War, Gan had become firmly attached to the Communist Party and worked in various official bodies for the next few years. Apparently, he was also briefly involved with Komfut (*Kommunisty-Futuristy* – the Communist-Futurists group) which had been established in 1919.[52] On 13 January 1921 he attended a Komfut meeting,[53] which seems to have been one of several unsuccessful attempts to resuscitate the organisation.[54]

In early 1919, Osip Brik invited Gan to join the Department of Fine Arts within Narkompros (*Otdel izobrazitel'nykh iskusstv* – IZO).[55] It seems that in this connection Gan attended the Museum conference in Petrograd[56] and became one of the editors of the journal *Art* (*Iskusstvo*). At this point, he was friends with everyone – precisely because he was not an artist, but was sympathetic to the experiments of the avant-garde, had a revolutionary background and was well versed in Marxism. Stepanova observed that he was straightforward, honest, "loves art" and did not engage in intrigues.[57] On 11 January 1919, Malevich and Rodchenko quarrelled over the fact that Olga Rozanova's posthumous exhibition had been decorated with Suprematist elements, but Gan did not take sides.[58] Similarly, in the late 1920s, when he was editing *Contemporary Architecture*, or *SA* as it was usually called, he published works by Malevich and Rodchenko, although to some extent they were occupying rival camps by this stage.[59]

In view of the later splits within the Russian avant-garde and the conflicts that arose between Constructivism and Suprematism, it is perhaps important to mention that Gan kept in touch with Malevich, even after the latter went to Vitebsk in November 1919.[60] Gan evidently valued the artist's work, regarding him as "a great and eminent figure", as well as "a straightforward and honest person".[61] In 1920, Gan organised Malevich's Moscow exhibition and produced wall texts, which reveal that he had read Malevich's brochure *From Cubism and Futurism to Suprematism: The New Pictorial Realism*, because he explained the artist's focus on "weight, speed and movement".[62] Gan seems to have collected the exhibits single-handedly, and was accused of not returning the work promptly.[63] In honour of the association between the two men, Malevich made Gan a member of his Unovis group (*Utverditeli novogo iskusstva* – Champions of the New Art), in Vitebsk, although Gan apparently declined to become involved.[64] Subsequently, Malevich calmly wondered how Gan would define "constructive art" now that he had founded the Constructivists.[65] Although Malevich became vehemently critical of Constructivism, he seems to have retained a relationship with Gan. When Malevich was moving from Vitebsk to Petrograd 1921-1922, he stored some of his works in Gan's studio.[66] For his part, Gan continued to respect and admire Malevich, acknowledging the importance of Suprematism for the genesis of Constructivism in the 1922 manifesto "Who We Are. Manifesto of the Group of Constructivists", written with Rodchenko and Stepanova.[67] Gan remained loyal to his old comrade and, in the late 1920s, when Malevich was being attacked for his formalism, Gan supported him by publishing his texts in the journal *SA*, as well writing an article about the inventor of Suprematism in which he emphasised the value of the artist's abstract experiments for those who were currently trying to develop new forms in architecture. He asserted, "the novelty, purity and originality of abstract Suprematist compositions will undoubtedly cultivate a new psychology of the perception of volumetric and spatial masses."[68] Even later, in 1929 when Malevich's large retrospective exhibition opened at the State Tretyakov Gallery in Moscow, to a deafening silence in the Russian press, Gan reviewed it positively, emphasising the way in which Malevich was exploring "the language of painting" in his work and pursuing his task with honesty and dedication.[69]

The Working Group of Constructivists

Gan's strong ideological commitment to the Revolution, the masses and the building of the new communist way of life expressed itself not only in his theatrical activities but also in his increasing involvement in art. He was clearly aware of the post-revolutionary debates that had been occupying avant-garde circles concerning the nature of the new art, the artists' desire to embrace industry, technology, science and the machine as the governing characteristics of the new workers' state, the notion of synthesising the arts as manifest in the design sketches that Rodchenko and others produced for *Zhivskul'ptarkh* (*Zhivopis' skul'ptura arkhitektura* – Painting, Sculpture and Architecture group), and the overwhelming desire to fuse art and life, which had been temporarily achieved when art had taken to the streets in the decorations and the mass spectacles for the revolutionary festivals.

In January 1920, Gan seems to have embarked on a more intensive study of art history and bought Stepanova's copy of Igor Grabar's *The History of Russian Art*, subsequently reading Mikhail Larionov's texts about Rayism and Malevich's Suprematist writings.[70] Gan even realised that Larionov had been talking about non-objective art as early as 1913.[71] Apparently, Gan often discussed artistic matters (including art's relationship to the Revolution) with Rodchenko and Stepanova. In early January 1920, the latter reported Gan saying that, "our art … is not proletarian, for it possesses no ideology, but only develops on the level of professional achievements".[72] At this time, the three were also thinking of organising "a group of innovators of all kinds of art".[73] This may represent the first emergence of the idea of setting up the Working Group of Constructivists, and certainly Gan's description of the group's genesis implies a strong personal basis for its emergence:

> The abstract painter Aleksandr Rodchenko, the painter Varvara Stepanova (Varst) and the constructor of "Mass Action" Aleksei Gan, having discussed the position of objects in art in connection with the social revolution and, seeking a social basis for the new trends, decided that art should be divided into two main currents according to fundamental criteria: firstly – art would continue the line of speculative activity of aesthetic creative work, which is known to unconsciously reflect reality; secondly – art would enter onto the path of real and active social reconstruction and would seek a socially meaningful and purposeful form of artistic work …
>
> Aleksandr Rodchenko's transition from the abstract planar compositions of "abstract creations" to abstract objects in real space; the pictorial schematisation and mechanisation of the human figure in the works of Varvara Stepanova; and finally, the materialistic construction of active culture by Aleksei Gan in opposition to the idealistic hysterics of theatrical actors, united them on the basis of the productive tasks of

> conscious artistic work. The former [Rodchenko and Stepanova], working in the field of fine art, went from compositions (an aesthetic sign) to constructions (the industrial principle), the second [Gan] having exposed the priestly magic of theatrical enchantment (dramatic art), moved to the problem of organising and consolidating the way of life of the workers' society (mass action).[74]

Indeed, both practically and conceptually, Constructivism's fusion of the formal (i.e. artistic) and the ideological was personified in the association between the ideologue Gan and the artists Rodchenko and Stepanova. Gan's account cited 13 December 1920 for the creation of the Working Group of Constructivists.[75] This probably represents the informal beginnings of the group, when the three of them decided on this course of action, but the group was not officially organised until March 1921 within Moscow's Institute of Artistic Culture (*Institut khudozhestvennoi kul'tury* – Inkhuk). Along with the three leaders, the other members were the artists Karl Ioganson, Konstantin Medunetskii, and the brothers Georgii and Vladimir Stenberg. Gan wrote the programme, although he was not present at the group's inaugural meeting, on 18 March 1921.[76] On 28 March, he introduced his work plan by emphasising that at present the artists were "working on material haphazardly" and "in a narrow professional way … artificially cut off from life", when what they should be doing was tackling the tasks of communist culture.[77] It is clear from the ensuing discussion that he was responsible for the terms used in the group's programme and for trying to create a coherent theory from the artists' rather vague ideas and aspirations.[78] Although his programme was ultimately accepted on 1 April 1921, there remained a great deal of divergence within the group over precise meanings and specific details.[79]

The group's (or rather Gan's) programme proclaimed a new synthesis of art and industry. It asserted that the Constructivists wanted to relegate their purely artistic explorations to the role of "laboratory work", and to extend their experiments with manipulating three-dimensional abstract forms into the real environment by participating in the industrial manufacture of useful objects.[80] They called this new type of activity "intellectual production", proclaiming that their ideological foundation was "scientific communism, built on the theory of historical materialism" and that their ultimate goal was "the communistic expression of material structures", which they hoped to attain by organising their material according to the three principles of *tektonika* ("tectonics", or the socially and politically appropriate use of industrial material), *construction* (the organization of this material for a given purpose) and *faktura* (the conscious handling and manipulation of it).[81] These principles embodied the artists' commitment to communism, industrial production and manipulating materials in accordance with the experience gained from creating works of art.

Gan emphasised five important terms in the "Programme of the Working Group of Constructivists": the word Constructivist, which denoted the new kind of creative figure; the concept of "intellectual and material production" which conveyed a new type of creative activity (corresponding to what we today call design); and the three principles that governed this new type of activity – tectonics, *faktura* and construction, which constituted the practical and theoretical basis of Constructivism.

Constructivism 1922

In 1922 Gan elaborated these ideas in his book *Constructivism*,[82] devoting a high proportion of his text to elucidating and amplifying the principles underlying the Constructivist approach. While the terms *faktura* and construction were already present in contemporary artistic discourse, the term tectonics or *tektonika* in Russian represented a new component in creative activity. This term, which was the first of the principles discussed in the book, had clearly been coined by Gan to encompass the ideological and industrial ethos of Constructivism and embodied the fusion of these concerns with the formal and purely artistic work that had preceded the emergence of the movement.

Prior to 1921, the term *tektonika* had been employed in conjunction with *arkhitektonika* (akin to the English architectonics and the German *Tektonik*), both of which derived from the Greek and both of which concerned the nature of harmony in the construction of buildings. Such qualities could also be applied to the other arts, as was indicated when the artists Aleksandr Grishchenko and Aleksandr Shevchenko used it in their statement of 1919 concerning "tectonic primitivism".[83] Of course, they may have been using it in the sense of Heinrich Wölfflin's "tactile values" (*tektonisch* in German), which, not surprisingly, seems to have been translated into Russian as *tektonika*.[84] The use of the term in artistic discourse was certainly not unprecedented. While its structural connotations might have prompted Gan to adopt the word, he disengaged it from its art-historical context and extended its remit to embrace wider and more explicitly political and technological considerations. In expanding its meaning, he was clearly influenced by its use in geography to denote the surface of the Earth.[85] He wrote in *Constructivism*, "The word 'tectonics' is taken from geology, where it is used to define the eruptions coming from the Earth's core."[86] This suggested that for him, it also possessed the ability to change the nature of artistic activity in a radical way. He stressed, "Tectonics is a synonym for the organic, for the upsurge from the inner essence."[87]

Gan may also have been inspired by the fact that *tektonika* sounds fairly similar to the Russian *tekhnika* and *tekhnologiya*, the Greek-rooted terms for technique and technology, an affinity, which gives *tektonika* a certain scientific ring.[88] It is also highly likely, as Kristin Romberg has suggested, that Gan may have employed "tectonics" in response to the way Aleksandr Bogdanov had used the term *tektologiya* or techtology during the 1910s to suggest the interconnection between different scientific spheres.[89] Gan was well acquainted with Bogdanov's writings, which he cited at length in *Constructivism*, and he was also using *tektonika* as a means of fusing various realms of activity, in very much the same way as Bogdanov had employed *tektologiya*.

Whatever the actual derivation of *tektonika*, Gan imbued it with a very specific ideological resonance. He defined it thus: "Tectonics or the tectonic style is organically smelted and forged from the qualities of communism itself on the one hand, and from the purposeful use of industrial material on the other."[90] In other words, tectonics represented the way that the requirements of communism, the industrial process and the practical demands of utility would be taken into account during the design process. In this respect it was fundamental to Constructivism. Gan stressed:

> As a discipline, tectonics must lead the Constructivist in practice towards synthesising the new content with the new form. He must be a person educated in Marxism, who has completely rejected art and really got to grips with industrial material. Tectonics is his lodestar, the reasoning behind his experimental and practical activity. Constructivism without tectonics is like a painting without colour.[91]

For Gan, tectonics denoted the process of synthesising artistic experience with the principles of communism, society's needs, and the practical requirements of working with mass manufacturing in actual factories. This was a demanding discipline. Not surprisingly perhaps, Stepanova, as a practising

Художественная культура, как одна из формальных выразительниц „духовной“—не разстается с ценностями утопических и грезовых видений, и ее фабрикаторы не отказываются от **жреческих функций оформленного кликушества.**

Коммунисты Наркомпроса, ведающие делами искусства мало чем отличаются от не-коммунистов вне-Наркомпроса. Они также находятся в плену у прекрасного, как последние пленены божественным.

Передатчики и популяризаторы, соблазненные жречеством, коленопреклоненно служат прошлому, на **словах обещая будущее.** Это их толкает в сторону самых реакционных, декласированных маниаков-художников: живописи, скульптуры и архитектуры. С одной стороны они—коммунисты готовые пасть в открытом бою с капитализмом при попытке какой бы то ни было реставрации; с другой—они как консерваторы, добровольно, без боя совершают падение, молитвенно благоговея перед искусством тех самых культур, **к которым они строго относятся, помятуя теорию исторического материализма.**

Ответственные высокоавторитетные руководители, к сожалению, сумбурно и безпринципно распоряжаются искусством не только вчерашнего дня, но и дня настоящего, и создают такие условия, при которых нет возможности коллективно и организованно поставить проблемы интеллектуально-материального производства на рельсы практического дела.

И не удивительно: они ведь плоть от плоти той самой тлетворной эстетики, против которой возстали материалисты-новаторы левого искусства.

Вот почему ведется и явно и тайно компания против „без'идейников" и „безпредметников". И чем содержательнее последние, чем нагляднее действительность говорит за них,—тем с меньшей разборчивостью с ними ведется борьба жрецами старого искусства.

Сейчас оффициально они—все, они задают тон и, как искусные лицедеи, гримируются под Маркса.

За ними не идет только пролетариат с его здоровым марксистским материализмом, но за то с ними многомиллионная масса: интеллигенты, агностики, спиритуалисты, мистики, эмпириокритики, эмпириомонисты, эклектики и прочие падагрики и паралитики.

Вот кто является ныне защитником

художественных ценностей

от имени коммунизма.

Constructivist, defined it in more pragmatic and less ideological terms: "When the static element of an object is replaced by purpose [a useful function], action and dynamics, this is tectonics".[92]

The second principle, *faktura*, seems to have been introduced into Russian artistic discourse by David Burliuk in 1912, as the Russian equivalent for the French term *facture*, denoting the texture of the painted surface.[93] Burliuk discussed it exclusively in relation to painting and particularly Cubism, referring to the smell of the painted surface, the sensual associations it generated (as an element of synaesthesia), and its tactile qualities (shiny and matt, smooth or rough, like metal, glass, or fabric, etc), and, as such, acting as a mediator between painting and sculpture.[94] *Faktura*, however, was soon expanded to include many different ways in which the properties and surfaces of all kinds of materials, not simply pigments, were manipulated, and exploited by artists. In 1914, Vladimir Markov (Voldemārs Matvejs) explored in minute detail the practical and philosophical ramifications of the term in relation to various phenomena, including sculpture, architecture, and icon painting, as well as nature and the machine.[95] *Faktura* denoted the way the materials became important expressive components in the work of art, as in Rodchenko's *Black on Black* (1919, Museum of Modern Art, New York), in which the artist used asphalt in place of traditional pigments in order to create a very different type of pictorial texture, and one that related the painting directly to the external world of building and construction.[96] Equally, *faktura* is integral to the kind of assemblages of rope, wire, glass, plaster, wood, and metal that Tatlin had begun to produce in 1914 and which he had first shown at his studio in May of that year.[97] In his *Model for a Monument to the Third International* (1920, exhibited in Moscow in Spring 1921), the smoothness and strength of metal could express not merely the individual sensibilities of the artist but also the power and might of the collective will of the industrial proletariat, while glass could communicate the transparency and accessibility of the new form of government for all.[98] In many ways, the meaning that Gan gave *faktura* as "the conscious choice of material and its appropriate utilization without interrupting the dynamics of construction or limiting its tectonics" corresponded directly with the practical example of Tatlin's monument and the identification between the proletariat and the machine that it celebrated.[99]

The third principle was "construction". The noun *konstruktsiya* (construction), from the Latin *constructio*, was well established in Russian usage by the end of the nineteenth century. Like its English equivalent, it could be used in a metaphorical way to describe the structure of language or society although it also acquired clear connotations of engineering, referring to the construction of buildings, technological structures, or machines.[100] By 1912, it had also become established in artistic discourse, since the Parisian Cubists Albert Gleizes and Jean Metzinger referred to construction in painting, "To compose, to construct, to design, reduces itself to this: to determine by our own activity the dynamism of form".[101] That same year, Markov adopted the term "constructiveness" (*konstruktivnost'*) to denote the rational, logical aspect of art.[102] In early 1919, the artist Ivan Puni used *konstruktsiya* in its strictly technical sense when he argued that artists should not be involved in industrial production: "What are the principles of a contemporary industrial construction?", he asked, and answered, "Its principle is maximum utility ... an artist does not have the right to interfere with the construction of an object, because an object simply will not be constructive [*konstruktivna*] if it is built according to the two [competing] principles of utility and aesthetics".[103]

Indeed, it was precisely because *konstruktsiya* carried these connotations that the terms "constructor" (*konstruktor*) or "artist-constructor" (*khudozhnik-konstruktor*) first appeared in an artistic context to equate the maker of art with a worker in industry. In 1918, when the avant-garde was discussing the nature of art in the new workers' state, they developed the idea that since the proletariat was the product of advanced industry, art itself should fully embrace the machine and industrial culture, and the artist should become "a constructor and technician".[104]

The adoption of the term *konstruktsiya* to describe the works of art themselves seems to have occurred at the same time or may even have been preceded by the coining of *postroenie*, from the Old Russian root *stroi* (a building, structure, or construct). This also had a broad range of reference in general usage, embracing building structures, the construction of geometrical figures, structures of language and thought, and even the construction of a socialist society.[105] In 1919, Popova referred to pictorial structure as *postroenie*, although she alluded to the strengths of the pictorial construction as *silyi konstruktsii*.[106] Similarly, in 1918 Rodchenko used the phrase "the severe, static structure of coloured planes" (*strogoe, nepodvizhnoe postroenie tsvetovykh ploskostei*) to describe his paintings.[107] By 1920, he was using the title *Konstruktsiya*, for works that consisted of simple or complex configurations of straight lines on plain grounds, in which a machine-like precision in the articulation of the surface and the linear construction emphasises the impersonal and analytical quality of the painting process.[108]

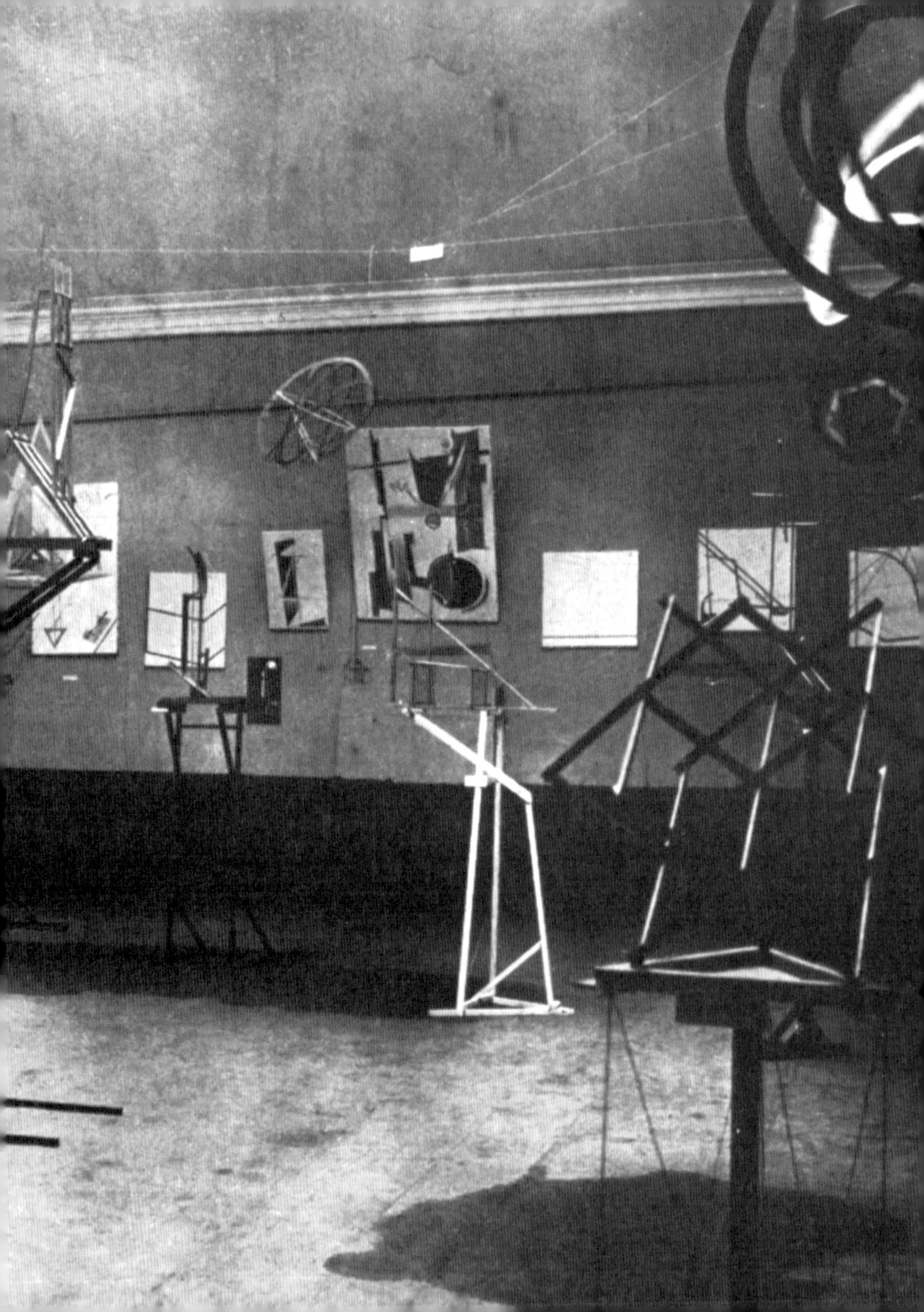

He also used it to describe the various architectural sketches that he produced for *Zhivskul'ptarkh* and ultimately for the open-work, three-dimensional structures that he made 1920-1921 and exhibited in May 1921 (p. XXXII). During the Composition/Construction debates within Inkhuk in the winter and early spring of 1920-1921, Rodchenko came to the conclusion that: "All new approaches to art arise from technology and engineering and move towards organisation and construction" and "real construction is utilitarian necessity".[109]

These three principles (tectonics, *faktura* and construction) lay at the basis of the new type of art, described as "material and intellectual production", a term that seems to have emerged out of the debates concerning proletarian culture, which dominated the post-revolutionary period. Gan himself related it to the declaration of the communist faction at the First All-Russian Congress of Worker and Peasant Theatres on 28 December 1920. According to Gan, this statement emphasised that "after the October revolution crushed the perpetual enemies of the workers and liberated us from political slavery and economic exploitation, we were confronted with a new task: to get rid of the spiritual captivity [prison] of the old world and get down to creating the intellectual and material [*intellektual'no – material'nye*] values of proletarian culture, through which we will advance towards universal human culture and the triumph of communism."[110]

Gan's book *Constructivism* was an attempt to explain, clarify, justify and promote the new creative approach. The earlier programme had emphasised the need to publicise Constructivist principles and develop strategies to secure government funding, such as arranging exhibitions (like that of May 1921), issuing a weekly journal, *The Herald of Intellectual Production* (*Vestnik intellektual'nogo proizvodstva*), as well as publishing "brochures and leaflets on the problems connected with the group's activities".[111] *Constructivism* was clearly an element in this strategy. Throughout the text, Gan emphasised the ideological nature of Constructivism, its political credentials, and its relationship to Marxism, even opening his exposition with an extract from the *Communist Manifesto* of 1848.

In the first half of the book, he took pains to place the emergence of Constructivism in an historical context, delineating the history of art in general and its relationship to society, arguing that Constructivism was an inevitable result of economic and social progress, just as Marxism itself was. In this respect, Gan's book was clearly conceived as part of the group's campaign to secure

АЛЕКСЕЙ ГАН.

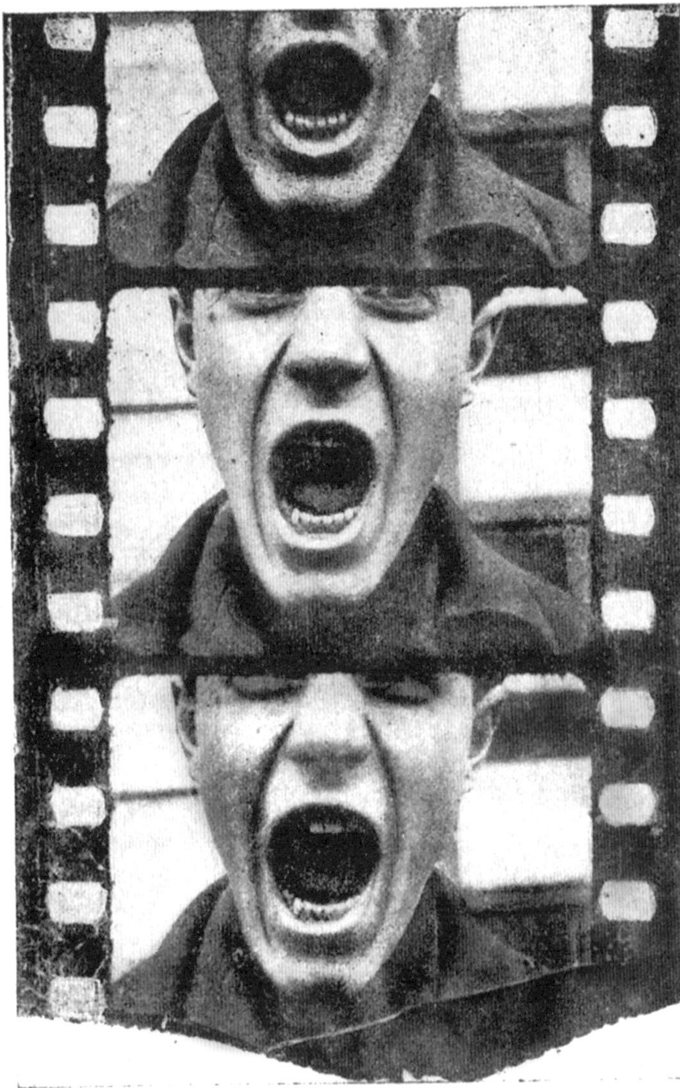

ДА ЗДРАВСТВУЕТ ДЕМОНСТРАЦИЯ БЫТА!

the support of the ruling Communist Party. The main thrust of its argument was that Constructivism represented the only truly revolutionary creative trend and therefore it alone should be adopted as the official aesthetic of the new state. Unwisely, Gan's impassioned pleas for government funding were accompanied by harsh criticisms of current Party policy towards the arts, which he castigated in no uncertain terms as reactionary and counter-revolutionary. It is not surprising perhaps that officialdom was not persuaded to support Constructivism.

It is typical of Gan's approach, however, that his theoretical exposition of Constructivism was closely connected with strategic thinking. It is also characteristic that the book itself, in its material form, was an agitational object, visually announcing the new approach, and acting as a blueprint for Constructivist graphic design, with its bold use of lines, different typefaces, innovative spacing, and presentation of slogans slung diagonally across the page like banners at a revolutionary festival. While the presentation of Constructivist principles in the design of the book's pages reinforced the detailed exposition of these principles on the pages within, such devices also produced "the maximum social and artistic effect", by conveying the quintessential message of the book even to the casual reader, who might do little more than glance at the pages.[112] In fact, Gan had no illusions that people would necessarily read every word, and he explained that in designing a book "It is essential to take into account the psychology of the reader, who is far from always reading a book, but frequently looks at it, and leafs through it."[113]

Extending Constructivism: *Kino-Fot*

Even before the publication of *Constructivism*, Gan had begun the process of extending the ideas of the new approach into the realm of the cinema and photography with his journal *Kino-Fot* (6 issues, 25 August 1922 – 8 January 1923), subtitled "The Journal of Cinematography and Photography",[114] and subsequently with his small book *Long Live the Demonstration of Life!* of 1923 (p. XXXIV).[115] In neither of these publications was the term Constructivism mentioned, but *Kino-Fot*'s connection with Constructivism was visually implicit in its pages, which were profusely illustrated with reproductions of work by Rodchenko and Stepanova, including images of Rodchenko's constructions that had been shown in May 1921 in the Constructivist section of the Obmokhu exhibition (*Obshchestvo molodykh khudozhnikov* – Society of Young Artists, p. XXXII).[116] Even more explicitly, issue number three included ten of Stepanova's drawings

КИНО-ФОТ № 3

ЖУРНАЛ КИНЕМАТОГРАФИИ И ФОТОГРАФИИ. ВЫХОДИТ ЕЖЕНЕДЕЛЬНО

19—25 сентябрь. 1922.

ПЕРВОЕ.

Пока разговаривают, что и как ставить на кинематографе, пока раскачиваются кино-производственники—кино-дельцы бойко торгуют старым хламом, рекламирование которого доходит до невероятных размеров цинизма.

Мы знаем целый ряд картин с измененными названиями, которые преподносятся, как новость, изготовленная в 1922 году.

Торговый капитал нагл и не любит перемониться.

Когда же он попадает в руки просто спекулирующих, он доходит до предельных форм лжи и обмана.

Всего несколько месяцев назад считали достаточным, чтобы надуть обывателя и сделать сбор—отметить на афише-плакате, что кино-картина только что получена из-заграницы.

Но этого стало мало.

Теперь нужно не только указание: «из-заграницы», а нужно сообщить—что именно и как это что звучит на Западе и в Америке.

Имя Чарли Чаплина сейчас является одним из тех, вокруг которого потирают руки господа спекулянты предвкушая обогащение.

В Р. С. Ф. С. Р. уже не один десяток демонстрировлся кино-картин «Чаплина» без Чаплина.

«Гибель Изверга», «Человек на пропеллере» и другие фильмы преподносились и преподносятся как фильмы Шарло.

Ходят слухи, что одна из прокатных контор уже имеет его трагедию-буфф «Дитя», которую она «выдерживает» до поры до времени.

Говорят, что «Кино-Москва» вынуждена была «сдать в аренду» на несколько лет Форум бывшему владельцу, чтобы приобрести всего Чаплина.

Все это происходит от того, что у нас мало, очень мало, серьезных и талантливых кинематографистов и наша кинематография пока что сплошь схватана цепкими и грязными руками кино-дельцов.

И странное дело!

Стоит появиться новому работнику на кинематографе, как «кино-спецы» поднимают вой и негодуют.

Но они удивительно милостивы по адресу новых кино-дельцов и всячески им покровительствуют.

Мы решили, чтобы остановить спекуляцию Чаплиным, посвятить ему, первому и единственному кино-комедианту, этот номер.

Пусть товарищи и граждане знают о нем больше, тогда труднее будет спекулировать кино-дельцам.

АЛЕКСЕЙ ГАН.

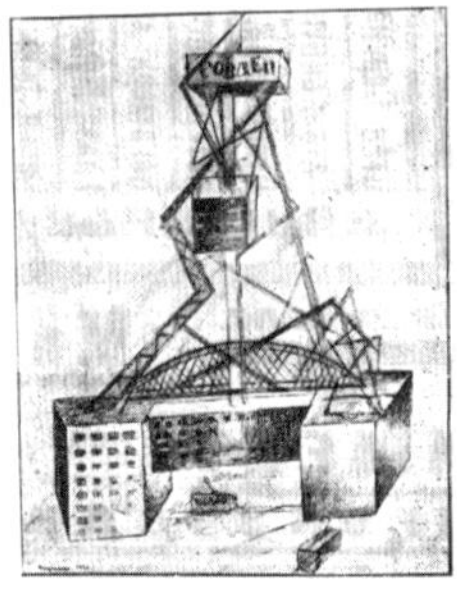

РОДЧЕНКО. Проект совдепа. 1920 г.

Чарли Чаплин.

Шарлотенбюргеры и Чаплинизм.

Письма, статьи, изыскания, поэмы,, интервью, портреты, стада подражателей и поклонниц, на лицо

! Чарли Чаплин en vogue. !

все признаки. Разверните любой парижский журнал или газету и вы наткнетесь на вести о Шарло. УЛИЧНАЯ ПРЕССА НЕУМОЛИМО ИЗОБРЕТАЕТ СВЕЖИЕ АНЕКДОТЫ И СПЛЕТНИ.

ВСЕ О ШАРЛО: биография, внешность, убеждения, меню, имя любовницы, отвращение к духам, все

занятное Шарлотенбюргерам: сплетни вблизи алькова, альковные анекдоты и очень мало о первом кино-актере Чаплине.

Западно-Европейская улица, не знающая удержу ни в восторгах, ни в ругани вопит так неистово, что и у нас начинают приглядываться к общему любимцу мира Шарло.

Почти десяток лет Чаплин в неизменном котелке на вз'ерошенной шевелюре и двумя точками усов у ноздрей являлся на наших экранах, он был героем тех фильм о которых возвещают:

ДВЕ В ВЕЧЕР

КОМИЧЕСКИХ

ГОМЕРИЧЕСКИЙ ЮМОР!

Сценарий Чаплина трудно озаглавить и общий ярлык—КОМИЧЕСКАЯ--тускнел перед патетической слизью психо-кино драм, с 10-ю строчным названием, «по Тургеневу» или цыганскому романсу, упоминавшим о «слезах, любви, розах, крови, страданиях» с неизменным участием горячих и холодных любимцев публики.

ЧАПЛИН ПЕРЕВОРАЧИВАЛ ВВЕРХ ТОРМАШКАМИ ПРИВЫЧНОЕ ПРЕДСТАВЛЕНИЕ О СЦЕНАРИИ, ОБ ИГРЕ, О ПСИХОЛОГИЧЕСКОЙ ДИЗЕНТЕРИИ, КОТОРАЯ ЗАПАКОСТИВ ДРАМУ, СТАЛА ИСПРАЖНЯТСЬСЯ В КИНО, его авторитет был отрицанием других вне, он явился раньше срока и был включен в ряд к[...] миков, последних в иерархии кино-благороди[...] Вот почему фильмы с Чаплиным не допускались [...] солидное кино, их местом были окраина и деш[...] вые «провёртографы».

В виденных мною 12—15 сценариях Чапли[...] отчетливо рисуется его роль в кино и даже театр[...]

Рис. Степановой.

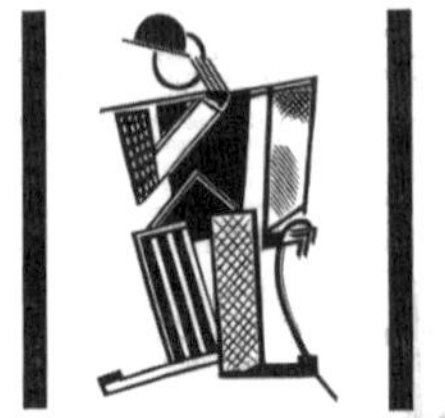

ШАРЛО НЕ МЕНЯЕТ КОСТЮМА И НЕ ДЕЛАЕТ ГРИМА

Предоставим Шарлотенбюргерам занимат[...] пышногрудой блондинкой-любовницей, бельем [...] задом Шарло, умиляться перед его выступлени[...] на балу в память Мольера.

Кстати, остроумная идея:

Почтить память

ПЛЯСОМ!

К сведению комиссии по орг. и т. д. и т. Островского.

Нам важен Чаплин—мастер, упорный работ[...] своего дела и те технические приемы, какими по[...] зуется он и все растущая группа его подража[...] лей «Чаплинистов».

ОТМЕТИМ ОСНОВНОЕ:

Чаплин не одинок, он скорей суммирует и [...] канчивает, найденное и начатое еще в серед[...] XIX в, английскими эксцентриками и клоунам[...] Все что пишет Зола о знаменитых бр. Ганло[...] Ли, применимо к Чаплину.

«Здесь (в пантомимах Ганлон-Ли) дубасят невинных и виновные осушают стаканы порядочных людей, здесь полное отрицание всякой справедливости, смелость оправдывающая преступления».

«Их сцены расчитаны по секундам... щелканье пощечин кажется стуком механизма в работе».

E. Zola: Le naturalisme au Théatre Par. 1913 p. 333.

Чаплин на экране всегда оппозиционен, неизменно угрожает благопозучию, спокойствию и **основным правам обывателей U. S. A.** Всякий сценарий—цепь эпизодов на эту тему. Везде веселый протест, везде зады и желудки отцов, полисменов и пасторов страдают от об'емистых штиблет Чаплина, всегда повергнутые в грязь, облитые водой, потные и вз'ерошенные представители семьи, власти и церкви теряют свой престиж и отступают перед самоуверенным шалопаем, путающимся в необ'ятных штанах.

Трудно дать название этим сценариям, еще трудней запомнить их содержание. Они вне обычной структуры.

Требование единства времени и места в развитии сюжета, давно сменено требованием единой линии его развития, ясности завязки, нарастания, конца и оправданности всех входящих предметов и лиц. Эта плавность развития уже чужда современности.

Рис. Степановой.

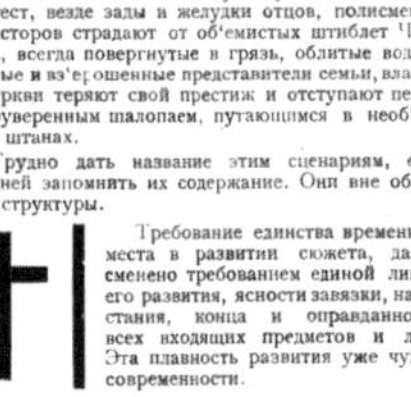

ШАРЛО УЕЗЖАЕТ.

Теперь переброска направлений взгляда (обострение внимания), перебой моторов, синкопа,—вся жизнь отрицает медлительную плавность.

Затем, обычные конфликты и их разрешение, ушли в обыденность—их минуют.

Плакат первый выдвигает воздействие контрастами. Взамен отжившего логического развития и психологической мотивации сюжета, Эренбург выдвигает термин: **тематический идиотизм.**

Рис. Степановой.

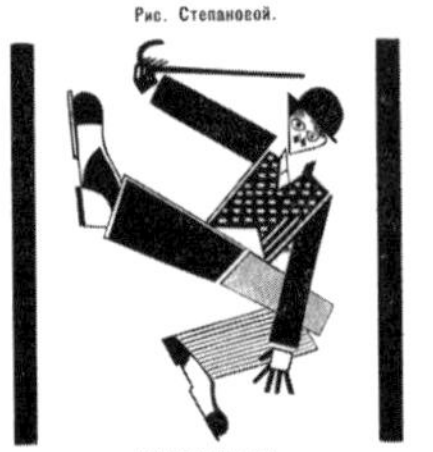

ШАРЛО ХОДИТ.

Сюжет развивается в контрастных перебросках, вне «здравого смысла» и норм психологии, в нем всегда перемены мест и точек зрения.

НАЧАЛО И КОНЕЦ НЕ ТОЖДЕСТВЕННЫ ЗАВЯЗКЕ И РАЗВЯЗКЕ.

Человек и предмет—равноценные части механизма намеченного сценарием.

Работа актера—работе механизма, его достоинства отчетливость и сжатость.

Игра Чаплина формулирует все найденное им и до него.

Чаплин всегда точен, он не знает жестов декоративных, ради жеста, в его работе всегда ясны направление и цель. Его игра вещественна, он реагирует только на вещи. Здесь немыслимо голое переживание, нельзя помнить о «глазах», о «профиле», работает все тело, весь механизм.

Чаплин разумно скуп в игре, он всегда концентрирует в одном месте выявление замысла, тем самым подчеркивая его. Всякая перемена движения имеет акцент, работа механизма—всегда учитывает зрителя, игра из кадра всегда «подается» в зал.

Его игра реальна—она правдоподобна и ясна, но в ней всякое движение приводит к неожиданным результатам.

Как и самый сюжет, игра Чаплина вне повседневной логики. В ней намечается ИЛЛОГИЧЕСКИЙ РЕАЛИЗМ, который станет основой в работах современного актера.

Игра Чаплина не позирование перед экраном, а совместная работа двух механизмов: кино-аппарата и кино-актера.

Рис. Степановой.

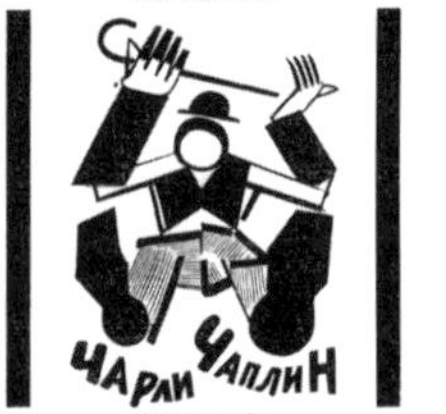

ШАРЛО ПАДАЕТ.

Заметка в каком-то английском журнале.

Знаменитый Чаплинский бег и отскок на одной ноге, являются примером такой комбинированной работы оператора и актера.

Отсюда несколько иной смысл приобретает анекдот в одном из последних №№ Paris le Soir!

!! **На конкурсе, в одном из театров, подражателей Шарло выступил инкогнито—сам Чаплин, и... оказался среди последних, недопущенных к окончательному состязанию.**

Ясно—имитаторы показывали результат работы Чаплина на экране, а он черновую, перед аппаратом.

ЧАПЛИН КАНОНИЗИРУЕТ НОВЫЕ ПРИЕМЫ, ОН АКАДЕМИК, здесь начало школы. Чаплин дает формулы, школа их развивает и популяризует. Американские комические картины, все идут под знаком «Чаплинизма».

Нам нужны его фильмы, этот наглядный курс «Чаплинизма», их нужно извлечь из мелких прокатных контор и сделать ряд «Чаплин-сеансов»—школой новых актеров кино и театра.

Н. ФОРЕГГЕР.

Если теперь...

Если в хламе теперешних кино-прокатных контор случайно находится какая нибудь завалившаяся комедия, вернее «комическая» картина, то любой театр охотно берет ее для демонстрации. Сейчас же выпускаются афиши, гласящие о том, что на экране такого-то кинематографа идет «комическая» выпуска 1922 г., с участием Чарли Чаплина. Если вы сейчас заглянете в любой иностранный журнал, то вы увидите, что о Чаплине пишут и говорят все. И в журнале для женщин, и в спортивном, и вероятно в журнале медицинском.

В Германии запрещают демонстрировать кар[...] ны с участием Чаплина. Интернациональное [...] щество «Дада» посылает Чаплину приветствен[...] телеграмму и протест против запрещения к дем[...] страции его картин в Германии.

Выпускаются Чаплинские монографии. Вся [...] ропа и Америка говорит о его последней карт[...] «Дитя».

В нашей кинематографически-нищей стр[...] мы чувствуем потребность в Чаплине, идем на [...] медии с Чаплиным и видим не последние, 192[...] фильмы, а старый прокатный хлам. Не настоя[...] го Чаплина, а подделку, так же похожую на него, [...] похожи остатки разрушенного двухэтажного [...] мика на нью-иоркский небоскреб.

Что же это такое за человек, что за удивите[...] ный натурщик? Почему нас к нему так тя[...] и почему он так знаменит?

Мы знаем, что на кинематографе не нужны те[...] ральные актеры, мы знаем, что обыкновенный чело[...] с совершенным механизмом своего обывательск[...] тела на кинематографе неприемлем. Нам нуж[...] необыкновенные люди, нам нужны «чудовища», [...] говорит один из первых левых кино работни[...] Ахрамович—Ашмарин. «Чудовища»—люди, ко[...] рые сумели бы воспитать свое тело в планах т[...] ного изучения его механической конструкции.

Чудовища, которые всю свою крепость, силу[...] героизм претворили бы в реальность, так необ[...] димую кинематографу, а не условность, для ки[...] матографа смертельную. Таких людей на кине[...] тографе можно пересчитать по пальцам. Та[...] прежде всего несравненный Чарли Чаплин, та[...] Гаррисон, такова Аста Нильсен, Гарри Карте[...] Диана Карен.

Рис. Степановой.

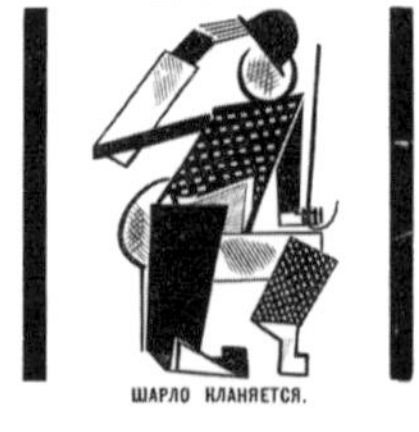

ШАРЛО КЛАНЯЕТСЯ.

И такова наша молодая крепкая закален[...] и чудовищная армия механических людей, экс[...] риментальная группа учеников Государственн[...] института кинематографии. Вот почему мы [...] любим Чаплина и вот почему его так не любят [...] кому дорога старая психологическая волынка [...] жденной от сифилитичного театра русской ки[...] матографии. Мы сейчас на основании точных

of Charlie Chaplin, one of which was used on the cover (front flap).[117] Indeed, the fact that Rodchenko and Stepanova designed the covers reinforced the connection between the new journal and Constructivism.

In *Kino-Fot* and *Long Live the Demonstration of Life!*, Gan linked the ideas of the Constructivists with the emerging theory and practice of avant-garde cinema. By connecting Constructivism with this dynamic new medium, Gan expanded the perspectives of the movement beyond the confines of art and design, providing and promoting a broad view of the Constructivist approach as one that would embrace all aspects of creative endeavour. This was an ambitious vision, but one that epitomised the aspiration of the revolutionary period to fuse art and life and to use creativity to promote the realisation of a communist society.

In *Kino-Fot*, Gan put forward the idea that the cinema (and by extension the static photograph, which was equally mechanically produced) should replace works of fine art such as paintings and sculptures, and take over their social and psychological role in meeting man's emotional needs. Gan's editorial for the very first issue declared:

> And everything that was previously done in an amateurish way by the arts of painting, sound and movement with the aim of organising our emotions is now automatically done by the extended organs of society – through technology, and in this specific case, by the cinema.
> Cinema as the quintessentially labouring apparatus of social technology, as the extended "organ" of society, is a matter for the proletarian state.[118]

In effect, this represented a slight, but important modification of Gan's position. The 1921 slogan "Death to Art"[119] now became "The new proletarian art is film and photography". In *Constructivism*, Gan stressed that "painting cannot compete with … photography".[120]

In fact, Gan was one of the first theorists to acknowledge the importance of photography and cinema and to recognise their immense aesthetic potential. Of course, Gan actually wanted photography and film to replace painting, and so ensure that painting as an outdated genre would not be revived. He was also undoubtedly affected by the importance that Lenin and the Party attributed to cinema and film. In 1919, Anatolii Lunacharskii, the Commissar of Enlightenment, had emphasised the power of film to disseminate ideas, touch the emotions and

счетов и экспериментальных работ изучаем человеческое тело, как механизм и не только потому, что мы эстетически любим машины, а потому, что человеческое тело действительно—механизм. Мы строим новую кинематографическую армию убийц Руничей, Стрижевских, Максимовых и прочих «кино-героев». И Чарли Чаплин наш первый учитель. То, что он процветает и то, что он могуч, это—лучшее доказательство правильности нашей линии, которую Чарли Чаплин интуитивно угадал, потому что он талантливый человек.

Нам некогда взвешивать свою одаренность, мы не знаем, талантливые ли мы люди, но мы знаем ценность точного расчета в кинематографической работе и необходимость зас'емки настоящих людей, а не «холодных» маринадов из «Стрижевщины», «Максимовщины» тож. И поэтому мы все любим Чаплина, ибо он нам близок, понятен и дорог.

ЛЕВ КУЛЕШОВ.

ШАРЛО.

— Он никого не изображает,

— Ничего не переживает,

— Редко меняет костюмы,

— Не делает грима,

— Всегда остается самим собой, ни над кем не издевается.

Он просто умеет показывать самого себя настолько полно и нагло, что действует на зрителя больше других.

Рис. Степановой.

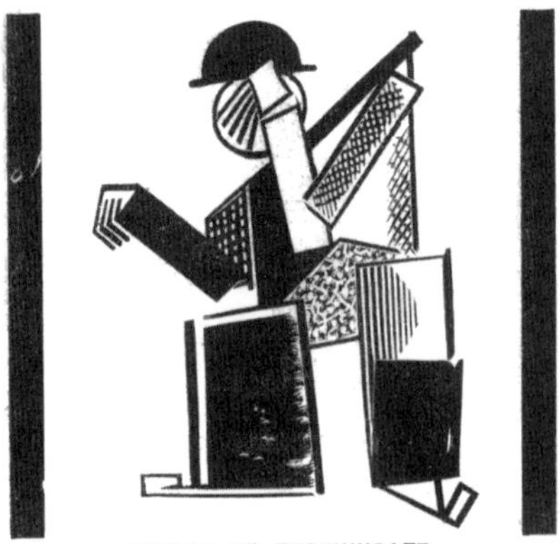

ШАРЛО НЕ ПЕРЕЖИВАЕТ.

Темп его движений контрастен темпу его партнера. Он не играет, а—ходит, бегает, падает—берет вещи, их разворачивает и показывает, как показывает и разворачивает самого себя.

У него нет пафоса, нет монументальности—в этом его ценность современности, он моментален.

Рис. Степановой.

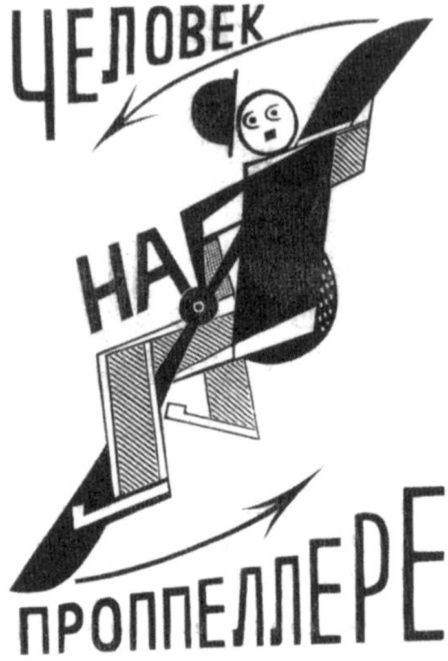

Ему не надо старой мишуры сцены—декораций, и новой мишуры—эклектического всеобщего конструктивизма наших монументальников с их богами: динамо, аэро, радио-станций, под'емных кранов и прочего.

Он—Чарли Чаплин—может показать все, что нужно на своем котелке и палке.

ЧАРЛИ ЧАПЛИН

был в цирке и знает, что вещи должны быть или меньше, или больше человека, что около горы или дирижабля человек ничтожество, но у винта и одной плоскости мастер ее.

Его колоссальный под'ем в точности и четкости—результат острого отношения к современности—войне, революции, коммунизму.

Каждый мастер-изобретатель возбуждается на выдумку новым событием или потребностью.

КТО СЕГОДНЯ? | Ленин и техника

— то и другое он принимает за основу работы.

Рис. Степановой.

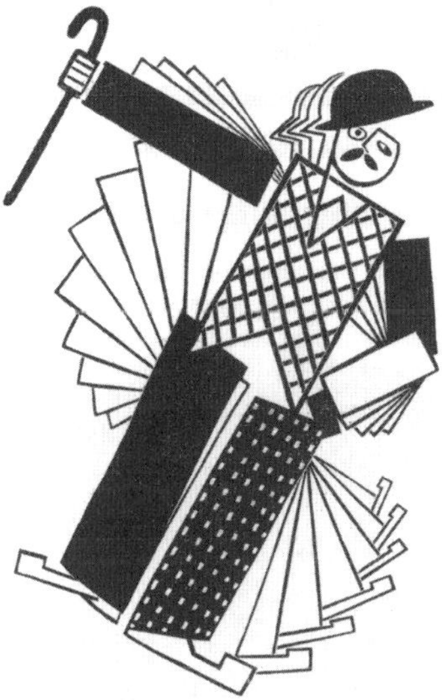

потеряли цену себе, цену взмаха руки.
Опоенные идеологией прекрасного, они не знают чистоты

надевания котелка —

походки человека

они узнали,

ЧТО ПРОСТО НИЧЕГО—ОБЫЧНОСТЬ, СТОИТ ВЫШЕ НАПЫЩЕННОСТИ и ЗАПУТАННОСТИ УМОЗРИТЕЛЬНЫХ ИДЕОЛОГИЙ.

Шарло всегда сам,—и только обыкновенный Чарли Чаплин. —

РОДЧЕНКО.

Так оформляется новый человек— мастер деталей т. е. будущий всякий человек.

Это сегодня—художник и актер Чарли Чаплин—мастер деталей.

МАСТЕР МАСС —

Ленин	и	Эдиссон
коммунизм	и	техника.

ЗАЧЕМ ОН НУЖЕН —

ЯСНО:

500.000.000 человек

Рис. Степановой.

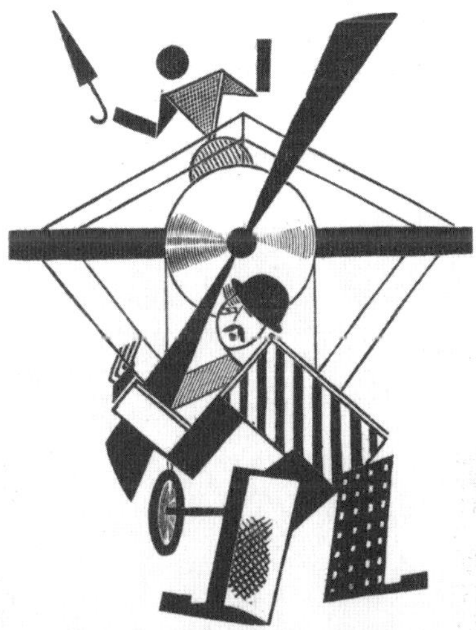

„КИНО-КОЛОСС“.

Большой зал консерватории.

Демонстрация кино-картин по четвергам, пятницам, субботам и воскресеньям.

become an apparatus of agitation.[121] Such ideas were enshrined in Lenin's "Directive on Cinematic Affairs", which became law on 17 January 1922, just over six months before Gan published his statement in *Kino-Fot*. The Bolshevik leader had aimed to create a Soviet film industry that would effectively inculcate Communist values through newsreels and propaganda films. The directive had also embraced photography, stipulating that "photographs of propaganda interest should be shown with the appropriate captions."[122]

Gan's assertion concerning the relevance and significance of photography as a propaganda medium and ideological tool may have played a role in encouraging the way in which photography came to such prominence in the activity of Constructivists like Rodchenko during the 1920s.[123] Despite Gan's important theoretical step, and the dual emphasis of the journal's title, *Kino-Fot* actually contained only a few articles relating to photography, some information about important inventions, such as a machine for developing prints and the creative potential of ultraviolet rays, along with a small quantity of reproductions – although these were mainly film stills. Cinema dominated the publication. Clearly, this was because, for Gan, progressive film and its methodology could provide important guidelines for Constructivist photography and photomontage. In fact, the journal illustrated some of Rodchenko's first photomontages, with commentary.[124] This marked the artist's and Constructivism's first engagement with photomontage, and significantly the journal presented the new medium firmly within the framework of innovative cinematic theory and practice.

Gan's interest in cinema undoubtedly related to his wider cultural activities, but it was also probably stimulated by Esfir Shub, his wife, who in 1922 had joined the State Committee for Cinematography in the USSR (*Gosudarstvennyi komitet po kinematografii SSSR* – Goskino), where she edited films for figures like Sergei Eisenstein, eventually compiling her own montage masterpiece, the film *The Fall of the Romanov Dynasty* (1927).[125] Galina Chichagova recalled, "Gan lived at 39 Starokonyushennyi pereulok. Consequently, there, in that house, we met Esfir Shub, Sergei Eisenstein, Dziga Vertov and others. There we also met for meetings of the Constructivist group."[126] Indeed, *Kino-Fot* was not published by any official state organisation, but privately by Gan himself, with the help of his colleagues.[127] Its editorial office was the house where Gan lived, and as editor and publisher he had complete control, securing help, support and contributions from colleagues, such as the poet Vladimir Mayakovsky, the film-makers Lev Kuleshov and Vertov, the theatrical critic Nikolai Forreger, and the art critic and theorist Boris Arvatov.

Kino-Fot's main focus was cinema, and for a time it acted as the professional journal for the industry. Its coverage was comprehensive, including inventions and Western developments, the activities of Thomas Edison, the adventures of Harry Piel, Russian organisations, schools, and screenplays. More importantly, perhaps, *Kino-Fot* also acted as a forum for new ideas concerning film making. The very first issue contained statements of two of the foremost innovators: Vertov's "We: Variant of a Manifesto" and Kuleshov's "Art, Contemporary Life and CINEMATOGRAPHY".[128] Although there were differences between the two film-makers, they were united in rejecting the conventional theatrical element of commercial films and they shared a firm commitment to producing a new Soviet cinema based on the principles of montage, which they considered reflected the essential reality of the proletarian state.[129] Gan was clearly enthusiastic about Vertov's work, and especially admired the thirteenth issue of *Kino-Pravda*, which he regarded as "pure montage" and the epitome of Vertov's "successful attempts to join together various subjects into a single, agitational whole".[130] Rodchenko had produced the inter-titles for the film, and Gan reproduced these in *Kino-Fot* (pp. XLII-XLIII).[131]

Gan also published an article on the Norwegian pioneer of abstract film Viking Eggling,[132] which he reprinted from the Berlin-based journal *Object* (*Veshch'/Gegenstand/Objet*), edited by El Lissitzky and Ilya Ehrenburg, which had appeared a few months earlier.[133] In fact, Gan reproduced one of Eggling's drawings from *Object*, even duplicating the mistaken attribution to "Richard Eggling".[134] One can imagine Gan being impressed by the dynamic qualities of Eggling's approach, its originality, its rejection of narrative cinema and the "acted" film, as well as the way it suggested a synthesis between art and film that could act as a viable alternative to easel painting. Nevertheless, its emphatically aesthetic orientation and lack of ideological content may have been less attractive. In *Constructivism*, Gan had condemned the editors of *Object* (*Veshch'/Gegenstand/Objet*) for precisely this fault, for being unable "to tear themselves away from art".[135] It is even possible that Gan also conceived *Kino-Fot* as a dynamic challenge to his colleagues in the West – a model of the new type of art needed in the communist state.

Р. С. Ф. С. Р.

КИНО ПРАВДА

Тринадцатый опыт.

Тринадцатый номер Кино-Правды следует рассматривать, как тринадцатый опыт В. Ф. В. О. в кино-производстве.

Мы всегда говорили, что основная задача советской кинематографии, задача государства, которое находится в крепких руках рабочих и крестьян—задача фиксации революционного быта на экране.

Кинематограф проклятого капитализма,—кинематограф пахабного торга—идущий навстречу обывательскому удовлетворению, — кинематограф не наш и он нам не нужен.

Кинематография молодая и революционная,—об'ективно отражающая день за днем происходящее—нам необходима и мы только в этом плане должны работать.

Создать „Кино-Газету", „Кино-Журнал" в общем и целом „Кино-Слово" для масс — дело не легкое.

Уж больно замаран экран искусством.

Так называемые художественные постановки изуродовали почти весь людской кино-штат.

С этим штатом старых кино-спецев нужного не выполнишь.

Вот почему мы так горячо приветствуем молодую силу, свежего работника, который не зацапан потными руками прекрасного.

Работа Дзиги Вертова идет как бы по двум основным направлениям.

Попытки чистого монтажа (в №№ 5 и 6) почти осуществленные в десятой „Кино-Правде", и попытки об'единения разных сюжетов в одно агитационное целое.

Последнее особенно удачно в тринадцатом номере, где даже надписи удалось конструктивисту Родченко подать как сюжет.

Например:

ЛЕНИН

Во весь экран.

Экранное слово.

Говорящий кинематограф киноматографическим языком.

Надпись как электрический шнур, как проводник, через который питается экран светящейся действенностью.

И мы все—видим в фокусе, как жили и живут улицы, площади, витрины, плакаты...

и слышим как они—

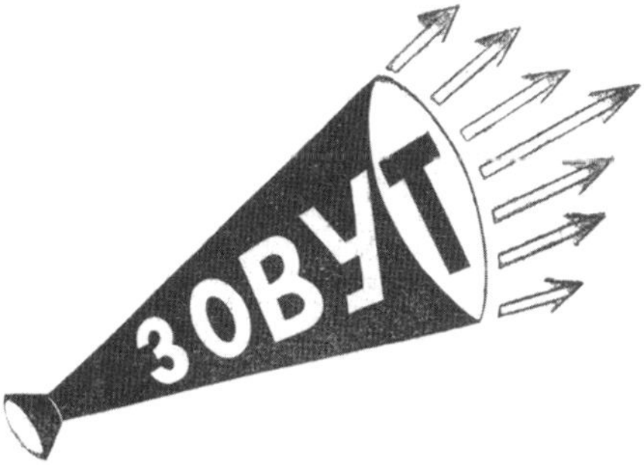

Всех, всех, всех!

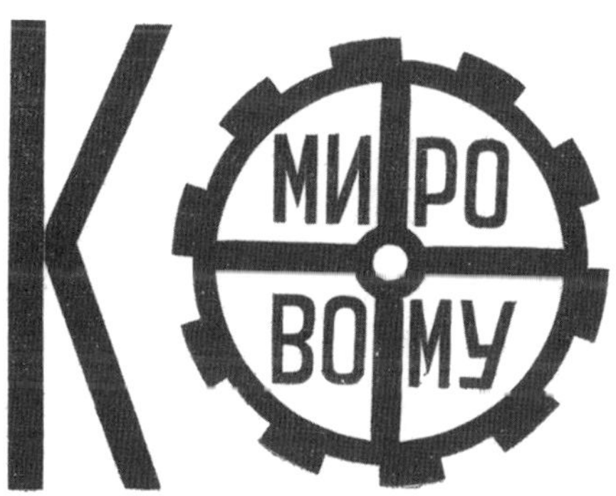

к пролетарскому

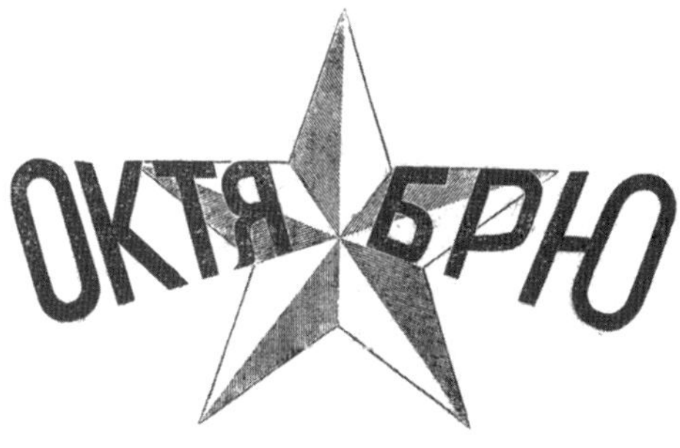

И мы видим аэропланы и одновременно смотрим с них вниз на землю, а земля бежит, несутся в новом плане улицы, дома, газеты и четкая с пространственным смыслом и временным тактом слова товарища Троцкого:

„Мы существуем, а они нас не замечают".

„Мы боримся", и боримся не на жизнь, а на смерть и не скрываем ничего.

Гробы в Астрахани, лопаты засыпающие тела наших погибших героев в Кронштате, склоненные знамена в момент погребения в Минске. Мы снимаем головные уборы. Это делают москвичи на набережной Москвы-реки.

Снова знамена врост и люди стремительно идут но Красную площадь.

Портрет рабочего Барболина, убитого в 1917 году.

Наплывает плакат

„Слава борцам".

А дальше разворачивается в спокойном монтаже: наши завоевания наша победа и наше неколебимое равнение на машину.

Да, великое дело кинематография!

Хороша тринадцатая Кино-Правда.

А. Г.

Натура Кино-Правды

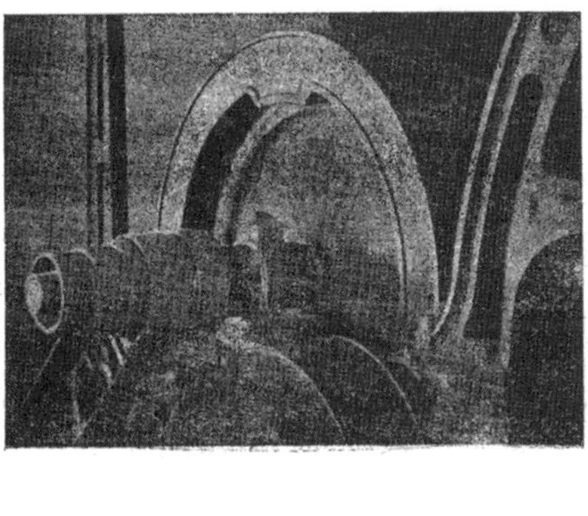

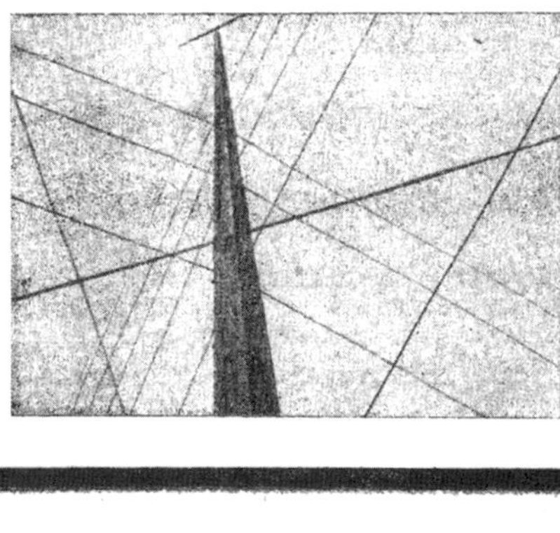

СА 3

СОВРЕМЕННАЯ
АРХИТЕКТУРА
ARCHITEKTUR
DERGEGENWART
L'ARCHITECTURE
CONTEMPORAINE

1928

АЛЕКСЕЙ ГАН

ГЛАВНОЕ УПРАВЛЕНИЕ НАУЧНЫМИ УЧРЕЖДЕНИЯМИ ■ ГОСУДАРСТВЕННОЕ ИЗДАТЕЛЬСТВО

Constructivism and Architecture: *Sovremennaya arkhitektura – SA*

As well embracing the theory and practice (including montage) of progressive film-makers, and allying them with Constructivism, Gan also promoted and assisted the emergence of a theory of Constructivist architecture. Indeed, Gan was one of the first people to start "rethinking the city as an active political agent in Marxist terms".[136] In *Constructivism* he had written about architecture, emphasising the need to discard the buildings and organisational principles of the old, capitalist city, because they were rooted in the economic and social life of the past. He argued that they were not only inappropriate, but they were positively harmful and "the staunch allies of counter-revolution"[137] because they actually impeded the reorganisation of the city that would foster the development of communism. One of Constructivism's tasks, therefore, was "to strip the bourgeois city bare";[138] another was to develop a new kind of architecture and urban organisation that would be able to foster the communist way of life. Gan insisted on the need to develop new architectural forms to assist in the creation of communism. The big question was what form the new architecture and urban re-organisation should take. Gan argued that communism was dynamic and it was in process of being established, therefore contemporary Russian society was in a state of transition, and the new built environment would have to take account of that situation and be flexible, so that as society moved towards communism, these new building would not impede its further development, but encourage it. He wrote:

> It is essential to teach ourselves how to build so that the dynamism of the product produced will not be an abstract or illusionary dynamism for visual impression, but an authentic dynamism of concrete movement.
> What does that mean?
> It means that if communism today needs a building for today, it must be provided, bearing in mind that tomorrow it will require a further form, and that this subsequent form must be supplied, so that it will not replace yesterday's form but supplement it, and in turn supplement the next form required.[139]

In his treatise *Constructivism*, and in a small article "The Communist City",[140] Gan had expounded the ideological basis for Constructivism in architecture, emphasising the social role of architecture and urban planning in realising communism. In *Constructivism*, Gan had also provided a clear explanation of Constructivist principles. He was not, however, an architect. The task of actually applying these ideas to the concrete process of design was undertaken by

СА

Цена 2 руб. 50 коп.

СОВРЕМЕННАЯ АРХИТЕКТУРА
ARCHITEKTUR DER GEGENWART

ТРЕТИЙ ГОД ИЗДАНИЯ

ОТВЕТСТВЕННЫЕ РЕДАКТОРЫ А. А. ВЕСНИН и М. Я. ГИНЗБУРГ

РЕДАКЦИОННАЯ КОЛЛЕГИЯ: М. О. БАРЩ, А. К. БУРОВ, Г. Г. ВЕГМАН, А. А. ВЕСНИН, В. А. ВЕСНИН, ВЯЧ. ВЛАДИМИРОВ, АЛЕКСЕЙ ГАН, М. Я. ГИНЗБУРГ, И. И. ЛЕОНИДОВ, А. С. НИКОЛЬСКИЙ (ЛЕНИНГРАД), П. И. НОВИЦКИЙ, Г. М. ОРЛОВ, А. Л. ПАСТЕРНАК, И. Н. СОБОЛЕВ

СОТРУДНИЧАЮТ: К. В. АКАШЕВ, I.P.P. OUD (РОТТЕРДАМ), М. О. БАРЩ, И. БЕЛДОВСКИЙ (ЛЕНИНГРАД), VIKTOR BOURGEOIS (БРЮССЕЛЬ), А. К. БУРОВ, Б. Н. ВАРГАЗИН, Г. Г. ВЕГМАН, А. А. ВЕСНИН, В. А. ВЕСНИН, Л. А. ВЕСНИН, И. ВИЛЬЯМ, HANS WITTWER (БАЗЕЛЬ), ВЯЧ. ВЛАДИМИРОВ, Н. ВОРОТЫНЦОВА, В. ГАЛЬПЕРИН (ЛЕНИНГРАД), АЛЕКСЕЙ ГАН, MAURICE GASPARD (БРЮССЕЛЬ), М. Я. ГИНЗБУРГ, И. А. ГОЛОСОВ, П. А. ГОЛОСОВ, WALTER GROPIUS (ДЕССАУ), И. С. ГУРЕВИЧ, А. П. ИВАНИЦКИЙ, А. Т. КАПУСТИНА, Г. КАРЛСЕН, В. И. КАШКАРОВ, С. Н. КОЖИН, Н. Я. КОЛЛИ, Я. А. КОРНФЕЛЬД, В. А. КРАСИЛЬНИКОВ, Г. Б. КРАСИН, KREIZAR (ПРАГА), А. КРЕСТИН (ЛЕНИНГРАД), KROHA (БРЮН), И. И. ЛЕОНИДОВ, С. Я. ЛИФШИЦ, А. Ф. ЛОЛЕЙТ, Г. М. ЛЮДВИГ, ANDRE LURÇAT (ПАРИЖ), В. МАЛИНОВСКИЙ (ЛЕНИНГРАД), MALLET STEVENS (ПАРИЖ), И. И. МАЛОЗЕМОВ (ХАРЬКОВ), С. А. МАСЛИХ, HANNES MAYER (БАЗЕЛЬ), И. Ф. МИЛИНИС (ХАРЬКОВ), MIES VAN DER ROHE (БЕРЛИН), И. И. МУРАВЬЕВ, А. С. НИКОЛЬСКИЙ (ЛЕНИНГРАД), А. А. ОЛЬ (ЛЕНИНГРАД), Г. М. ОРЛОВ, М. П. ПАРУСНИКОВ, А. Л. ПАСТЕРНАК, Р. ПОЛЯК, С. Л. ПРОХОРОВ, М. СИНЯВСКИЙ, И. Н. СОБОЛЕВ, А. С. ФУФАЕВ, Н. В. ХОЛОСТЕНКО (КИЕВ), Н. ЧУЖАК,

Главлит № А—6374. Типография Госиздата „Красный пролетарий". Москва, Пименовская улица, 16. Тираж 2.500 экземпляров

СА

1

ОТВЕТСТВЕННЫЕ РЕДАКТОРЫ: А. А. ВЕСНИН и М. Я. ГИНЗБУРГ

РЕДАКЦИОННАЯ КОЛЛЕГИЯ: М. О. БАРЩ, А. К. БУРОВ, Г. Г. ВЕГМАН, А. А. ВЕСНИН, В. А. ВЕСНИН, ВЯЧ. ВЛАДИМИРОВ, АЛЕКСЕЙ ГАН, М. Я. ГИНЗБУРГ, И. И. ЛЕОНИДОВ, А. С. НИКОЛЬСКИЙ (ЛЕНИНГРАД), П. И. НОВИЦКИЙ, Г. М. ОРЛОВ, А. Л. ПАСТЕРНАК, И. Н. СОБОЛЕВ.

МАКЕТ СДЕЛАЛ И. И. ЛЕОНИДОВ

REDIGIERT VON: M. J. GINSBURG UND A. A. WESNIN

REDAKTIONSKOMITÈE M. BARTSCH, A. BUROFF, ALEXEJ GAN, M. GINSBURG, I. LEONIDOFF, A. NIKOLSKY, P. NOWITZKY, G. ORLOFF, A. PASTERNAK, I. SSOBOLEFF, G. WEEGMAN, A. WESNIN, V. WESNIN, W. W. WLADIMIROFF

AUSSTATUNG UND DRUCK VON I. LEONIDOFF

ГЛАВНОЕ УПРАВЛЕНИЕ НАУЧНЫМИ УЧРЕЖДЕНИЯМИ. ГОСУДАРСТВЕННОЕ ИЗДАТЕЛЬСТВО

СОДЕРЖАНИЕ НОМЕРА.

Moisei Ginzburg and Aleksandr Vesnin. Ginzburg's own treatise *Style and the Epoch* (1924) elaborated Gan's precepts, especially those relating to ideology, function and technology, within an architectural context. Among his illustrations of structures pointing towards a new approach was Gan's book kiosk (p. LXIV).[141] The following year, Ginzburg and Vesnin together set up OSA (*Obedinenie sovremennykh arkhitektorov* – the Association of Contemporary Architects), which, in line with Gan's opposition to the speculative activity of art, discarded the idea of architectural style and focused on the development of the functional method. According to this, the form of a building would emerge from defining the functional spaces required for it to serve its purpose.

In 1926 Gan joined the editorial board of the association's journal *SA* (*Sovremennaya arkhitektura – Contemporary Architecture*, 1926-1930), and from 1926-1928 was responsible for designing its covers and layout (pp. XLIV, XLVI-XLVII, LIV-LV, LVIII-LIX and back flap).[142] Since much of the material consisted of drawn plans and elevations, or information about the latest techniques, it must have been fairly challenging to create visually arresting typographical designs. Yet Gan managed to do precisely this by using different typefaces at different scales and through his masterly placing of the images on the page – employing asymmetry and space to unite word and image, but also to generate dynamism, while retaining clarity and coherence.

Gan's work for *SA* extended beyond the visual organisation of the contents to contributing articles. Although some of these texts dealt with typography, or artistic matters, others dealt with architecture.[143] Gan, for instance, wrote about Mikhail Barshch and Mikhail Siniyavskii's Moscow Planetarium, welcoming it as a new type of theatre:

> Up to now, the theatre has been nothing more than a building in which cult services take place ... **Our** theatre must be different. It must inculcate a love of science in the spectator. The planetarium is an optical scientific theatre and represents one of the forms of **our** theatre.[144]

Gan also selected some of the texts and illustrations for *SA*. These materials did not always refer directly to architecture, but often related to the wider environment and broader issues concerning the organisation of everyday life in communist society. These items included Rodchenko's advertisements and his Workers Club of 1925, various pieces of furniture devised by Vkhutemas students from the Wood and Metal Work Faculty (notably A. Galaktionov, Bykov,

Morozov, N. Sobolev, Georgii Miller, and others), and even Gan's own kiosks.[145] These visual and textual components reflect Gan's commitment to publicising Constructivist precepts, his dedication to transforming every object within the environment, not just architecture, and his belief that the same universal principles could be applied to different design tasks in the great work of realising communist society.

While a lot of this material could be directly related to Constructivism, as a multi-disciplinary exercise, other elements seem to have much less direct bearing on Constructivist concerns and very little to do with "intellectual and material production". In particular, Ivan Klyun's text on "Cubism as a Pictorial Method" and Malevich's article on "Form, Colour and Sensation" possess very different creative viewpoints.[146] Both essays were published under the rubric "Discussion Section" (*Diskussionnyi otdel*), and in the case of Malevich to disclaimers that the editors understood the mystical nature of the artist, but they wished to demonstrate that "formal problems are not a self-sufficient foundation or starting point in designing the new architecture".[147] They clearly thought that Malevich would condemn himself and pointed out that they published his letter "despite the fact that certain parts of it are entirely incomprehensible".[148] Nevertheless, the editors also admitted that "The problem of architectural form, the significance of colour and questions of perception are very much on the agenda as far as we are concerned. The battle continues against representatives of eclecticism and those who express purely formal tendencies in architecture."[149] As this indicates, the inclusion of Suprematist material in *SA* suggests a certain degree of tolerance, but also perhaps a growing perception that the avant-garde needed to show some degree of solidarity given this "battle" and increasing official support for realism in painting and more traditional approaches in architecture. Of course, both these artists were old acquaintances, if not friends, of Gan's, having published texts in the "Creative Work" section of *Anarchy* in 1918. Indeed, in 1927, Gan had written about Malevich, stressing that although "his works do not have that concrete social utility, without which contemporary architecture is not architecture at all – they have very great importance as abstract investigations of new form as such".[150] Loyalty to erstwhile colleagues and a willingness to look at and harness the work of men who were not Constructivists (in whatever way) suggests that Gan was not a narrow-minded ideologue, but someone who was profoundly and sincerely concerned to use all kinds of expertise in order to create an environment and culture that would be worthy of the Russian working class and foster communism.

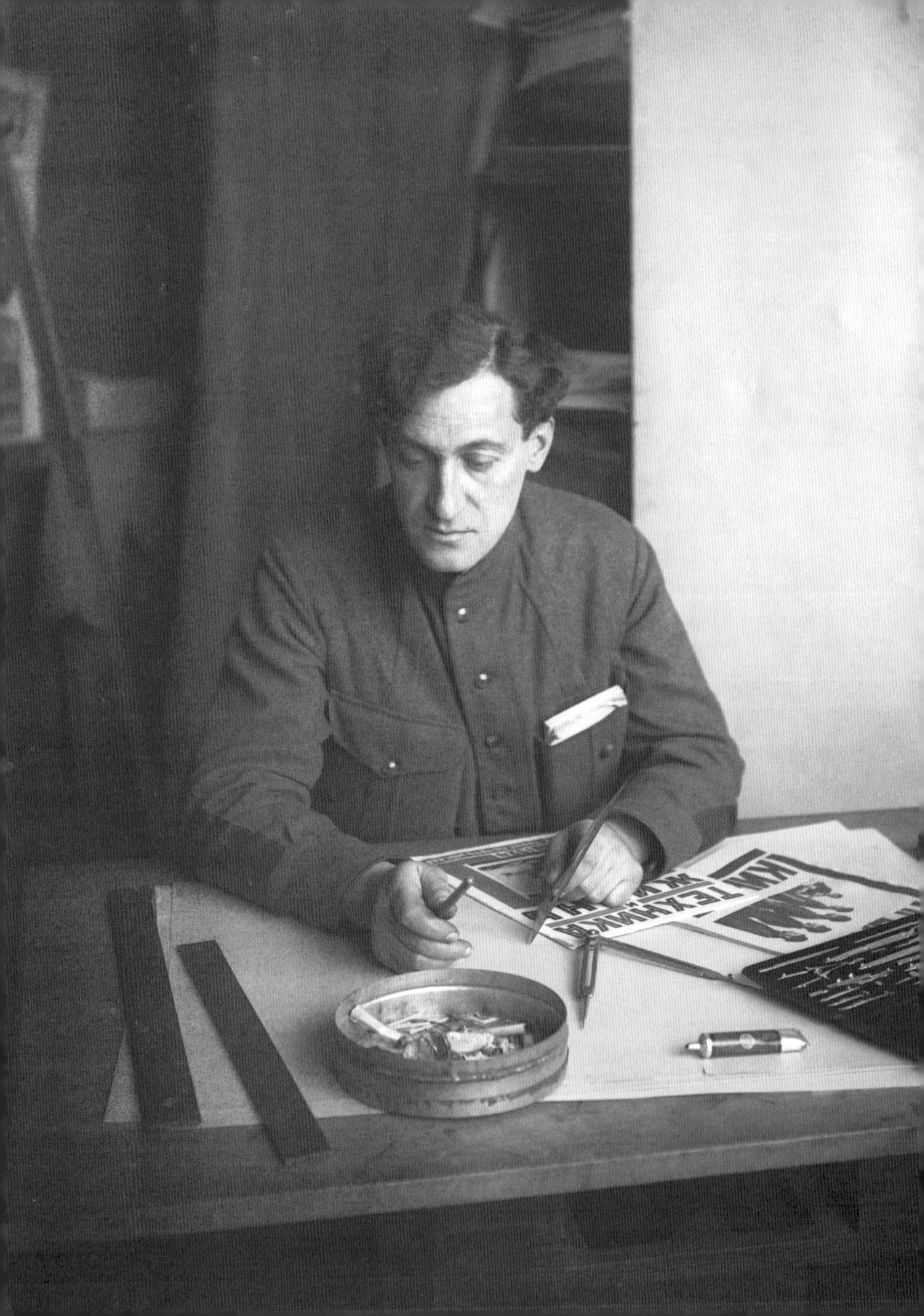

The Theory and Practice of Constructivist Typography

Gan was a prolific publicist, and was concerned to give his ideas visual impact. This concern seems to have lain at the basis of his work in typographical design. In fact, he played a crucial role in elaborating the theory and practice of Constructivist typography, which he connected firmly to the machine aesthetic, not only in appearance but also in essence. He argued that the Constructivist should use the pre-existing elements in a type-setter's or printer's arsenal. In this way, he tried to eliminate the hand-crafted letters and lines that were so typical of much early avant-garde typography. In their stead, Gan favoured the machine-tooled, precise as well as impersonal elements of existing typesetting. He called this "the mobilisation of typographical material",[151] which was part of the "transformation of the typesetting of text"[152] and "transformation of the type and linear composition".[153] By the time that he was designing the covers and layouts for *SA* in 1926, he felt that his theory and practice had fully developed. He wrote:

> In 1922 Constructivism entered the printing industry. Before this, the Constructivist, Aleksei Gan had composed a series of individual publications in which he had applied the principles of Constructivism, but he had not yet established a strict system of type-setting and typographical composition, which only now has emerged and been developed in a whole range of our major printing presses. From the transformation of the typesetting of the text and the activation of the typographical material (1918) [i.e. *Anarchy*], Aleksei Gan has gone on to organise the printed surface (1921-2) [i.e. *Kino-Fot* and *Constructivism*]. The next stage of work to be considered is the typification of the separate elements as well as of the complete, printed object as a whole.[154]

Ever since his editorial work for the "Creative Work" section of *Anarchy* in 1918 and for IZO's Wall Newspaper (*Stengaza*), in 1920, Gan had been concerned with the most effective way of presenting texts to the general public.[155] For Gan, the wall newspaper was "a form of mass work on the word", which "develops strong cadres of worker correspondents, in whose hands the word will become a powerful weapon for life-building".[156] He wrote:

> In practical terms, our revolution has given birth to the wall newspaper as an everyday necessity. The lack of paper, the destruction of printing workshops, the absence of raw materials, the decline in industrial

> power – all of this encourages the organiser's contemporary idea of producing with the minimum of expense and with beggarly means the maximum in terms of use ... but there is often not a sufficiently well-thought out plan or form.[157]

Gan had clearly tried to rectify these deficiencies in his own design work, and had evidently tried to make the "Creative Work" section of *Anarchy* more varied in terms of type-face, scale and spacing than the usual newspaper format of the time.[158]

Obviously, an important element in this need to make the word "a powerful weapon for life-building" was the actual typeface used. Gan was one of several figures who were concerned to develop a new typography that would express the essence of the new order. In early 1922, Popova had used thick, black and coloured lines and chunky lettering in her costume designs for Meyerkhold's production of *The Magnanimous Cuckold*, in her drawing of the set, and in the lettering she used on the wheel of the set.[159] In many ways, these lines and letters reflected the method of constructing the set, its emphasis on economy, and also Popova's use of linear elements in her paintings. Subsequently, Gan started developing these devices in his own typographical work, giving them a wider resonance in *Kino-Fot* and *Constructivism*.

Indeed, important strides in the consolidation of Constructivist typography were made during the spring and summer of 1922, when Gan conceived and published the magazine *Kino-Fot*.[160] As a whole, the covers for *Kino-Fot* develop the emphasis on the machine by exploiting the existing mass-produced means of the printing press. Gan seems to have designed the cover of the first issue himself, using large sans-serif lettering and thick lines as framing and organising devices above a photograph of a scene from Vasilii Toporkov's *Apple* (*Yabloko*) with the actor Sergei Komarov (front flap). Stepanova, however, designed the cover for the second and third issues, working within the format already created by Gan. Although the first issue had been completely printed in black, the colour red was introduced into the second issue: with the number "2" and "*anons*"(trailer or announcement) in red on the cover. These two elements of colour, along with Stepanova's drawing of Charlie Chaplin animated the design for issue number three, imbuing it with a sense of dynamism, in contrast to the rather static quality of the cover for the first issue.[161] Rodchenko produced the cover of the fourth issue using a photograph of Vladimir Mayakovsky as the hero in a still from the Russian film of Jack London's novel *Martin Eden*, which describes a poor seaman's pursuit of education and literary fame. The cover image shows the hero quarrelling with Death – comprising a skull and an aeroplane. Rodchenko's cover for the fifth issue of *Kino-Fot* represents a simple portrait of the American inventor Thomas Edison, who developed film cameras, projection equipment and even produced films. Gan himself designed the cover for the sixth and final issue which combines two images of a projector (printed in black) and a large red film reel, almost like a double exposure. This is an early use of this device, which became quite common in Constructivist and other modernist design. To the extent that all three leaders of the Working Group of Constructivists were engaged on designing the journal's covers, visually *Kino-Fot* represented a joint Constructivist enterprise.

The interior organisation of the magazine was equally inventive, using space and colour economically, but effectively. Gan tended to place his thick lines horizontally and vertically, using them as strong organisational elements, which possessed a substantial presence on the page. Text and image were placed, often asymmetrically, within this linear framework, which varied considerably from page to page (pp. XXXVI-XXXIX). Occasionally, Gan used a diagonal line, but usually dynamism was introduced by placement, the use of the space of the page as a positive element in the composition, and the use of different sizes of type and sometimes different type faces (pp. XLII-XLIII).

Not surprisingly, given her authorship of some of the covers, Stepanova advertised *Kino-Fot* and its Constructivist typography and content, by including it in her designs for Meyerkhold's production of *The Death of Tarelkin* (*Smert' Tarelkina)* of November 1922. The word "Kino-Fot" was printed on one side of a long paper ribbon handled by the bureaucrats on stage.[162]

In conjunction with his design work for *Kino-Fot*, Gan also devised the typography for *Constructivism*, which was conceived as an "agitational book" on several different levels. It was not merely a text publicising Constructivist ideas and approach, it also took (along with *Kino-Fot*) some of the first steps towards demonstrating how such ideas might be exploited in practical terms, and how they could be used to develop a distinctively Constructivist graphic design. In fact, *Constructivism* was the first book to display some of those visual features and typographical elements that would eventually come to be associated with Constructivist graphic design. Yet *Constructivism* is more of an experiment towards creating a Constructivist typography, than a fully-fledged realisation of Constructivist ideals and, in this respect, it remains unresolved as a book design.

ПЕРВАЯ ВЫСТАВКА СОВРЕМЕННОЙ АРХИТЕКТУРЫ

ERSTE AUSSTELLUNG DER ARCHITEKTUR DER GEGENWART

18 июня открылась Первая Выставка Современной Архитектуры, организованная Главнаукой и ОСА.

Две основные задачи надлежало разрешить выставке. Первая заключалась в том, чтобы противопоставить все еще господствующему в нашем практическом строительстве беспринципному эклектизму—единый фронт современной архитектуры. Вторая — в том, чтобы иметь возможность подвести итоги достигнутому, увидеть ясно все недочеты и наметить четкие дальнейшие пути к активному завоеванию нашей строительной действительности.

Первую задачу можно считать выполненной вполне удачно. Единый фронт современной архитектуры подтвердил свое существование. Работы Выставочного Комитета закрепили тесную связь между передовыми архитекторами Москвы, Ленинграда, Киева и др. городов СССР. Они обнаружили тот отрадный факт, что почти нет такого уголка Союза, такого архитектурного ВУЗ'а где не было бы большей или меньшей ячейки архитекторов-революционеров, горячо отстаивающих интересы подлинно современной архитектуры, в чрезвычайно тяжелых условиях безнадежного атавизма окружающей их среды. Выставка показала, что все усилия наших московских товарищей, находящихся в более благоприятных условиях, должны быть направлены на помощь и поддержку наших соратников других городов Союза.

С другой стороны, Выставка показала, что передовые идеи современной архитектуры, интернациональной в общих своих принципах, сильней тех пограничных кордонов и препятствий, которые создала послевоенная капиталистическая Европа. Выставка показала, что нет такой Европейской страны где бы не существовало большей или меньшей группы архитекторов-новаторов, противопоставляющих международному эклектизму и тупой реакции—новых идей современной архитектуры. И конечно совершенно естественно эти архитектора-одиночки, представляют собой самые прогрессивные слои Европы, проявившие исключительный интерес и доброжелательство к новой Советской России и в частности к ее представителям в области архитектуры.

Единый фронт современной архитектуры протягивает теперь свои нити от Парижа, Дессау и Берлина, Праги и Брюсселя к Москве, Ленинграду, Киеву и Томску.

Наша дальнейшая задача теперь—эти нити всемерно продолжать и укреплять.

Вторая проблема, которая должна разрешить Выставка—это итоги и выводы, результаты и перспективы. Проблема еще более важная и насущная. Ей редакция современной архитектуры отводит два свои ближайших номера, намереваясь как можно полнее представить все наиболее интересное из экспонатов Выставки и на базе этих экспонатов произвести учет сделанного и прогноз дальнейших путей.

Л. А. И А. А. ВЕСНИНЫ. ПРОЕКТ ГОСТИНИЦЫ В НОВОЙ МАЦЕСТЕ. L. UND A. WESSNIN. ENTWURF EINES HOTELS IN MAZESTA (KAUKASUS)

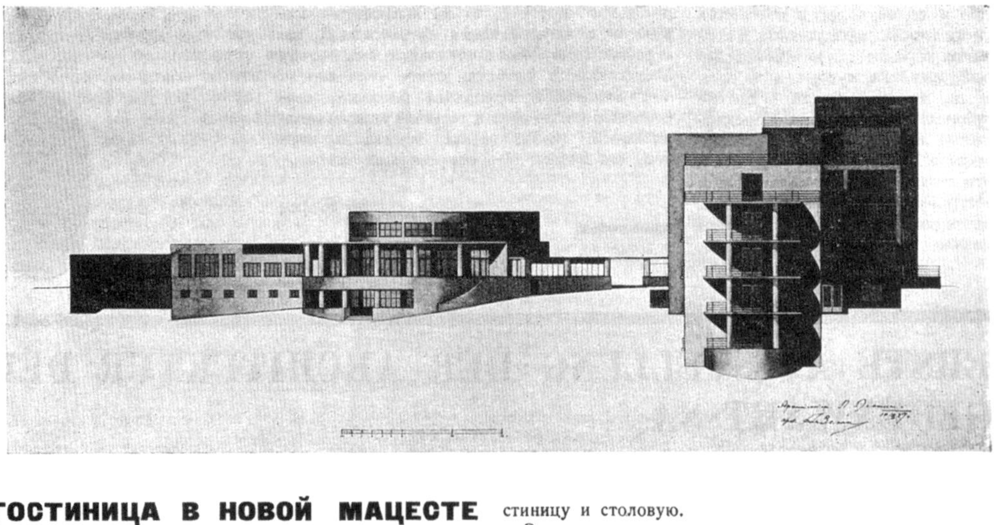

ГОСТИНИЦА В НОВОЙ МАЦЕСТЕ

Отведенный для постройки участок земли находится недалеко от главного ванного здания Новой Мацесты. Он обладает сложным рельефом местности и сравнительно крутыми уклонами горы, идущими к морю.

При выборе места для постройки гостиницы, пришлось учесть существующие площадку, дороги и подъезды. Здание гостиницы нужно расположить, группируя его около площадки, которая служит местом подъезда в гостиницу и столовую.

Здание гостиницы состоит из корпуса номеров, идущего по уклону горы уступами с севера на юг, и отдельного корпуса столовой и кухни, соединенных между собой крытым переходом. Столовая и кухня расположены вдоль горизонтали, ограничивающей площадку.

Главный корпус гостинницы включает 150 жилых номеров, из которых 50 номеров проектируются площадью по 12.0 m^2, 90 номеров по 16.0 m^2, и 10 номеров по 20.0 m^2.

ГЕНЕРАЛЬНЫЙ ПЛАН, АКСОНОМЕТРИЯ, ПЛАНЫ. LAGEPLAN, AXONOMETRISCHE DARSTELLUNG, GRUNDRISSE

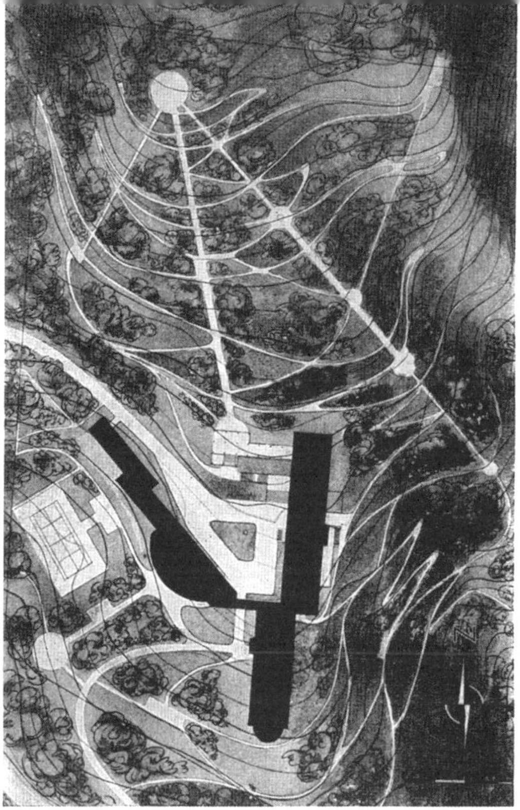

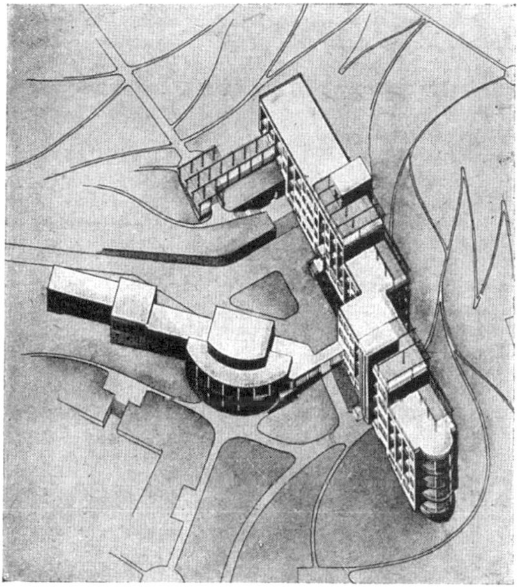

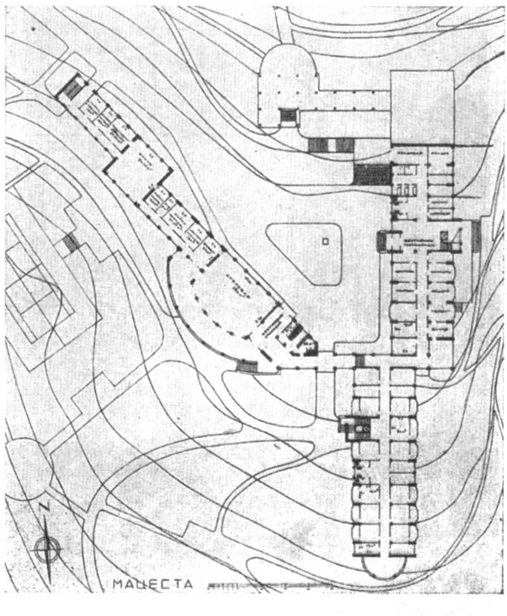

100 номеров имеют индивидуальные изолированные балконы, выходящие на восток и запад: остальные имеют террасы и веранды общего пользования. Вблизи вестибюля и перехода в столовую расположены комнаты отдыха и общего пользования.

Плоская крыша, идущая уступами и обработанная трельяжами, предназначается для приема воздушных и солнечных ванн.

Столовая проектируется как для обслуживания населения гостиницы, так и окрестных дач, имеет большую веранду, открытую к морю на юго-запад.

Здание проектируется железо-бетонное с устройством центрального отопления и вентиляции, с общей кубатурой около 20.000 m^3.

Весь участок гостиницы обрабатывается парковыми дорожками, площадками для игр и терренкурами с уклонами $^1/_{50}$, $^1/_{20}$ и $^1/_{10}$, ведущими к беседке отдыха, расположенной в верхней части парка

The cover includes the same kind of chunky, sans-serif lettering as we find in Popova's designs, but it also incorporates two different typefaces. Whereas Gan's name appears in the kind of lettering later associated with Constructivist design (at two different sizes), the word "конструктивизм" appears in a different, somewhat lighter typeface. It is also presented negatively, i.e. as white against the black of the rectangular box within which it is held. This device sets the precedent for the way that Rodchenko later placed Vladimir Mayakovsky's name in a white box against a dark ground for the cover of *About This* (*Pro eto*) of 1923.[163]

The experimental approach evident in the cover of *Constructivism* extended to the layout of the book's interior. The title page is fairly conventional, and a large number of the pages consist solely of closely printed typeface, although Gan varied the size of the typefaces and the spacing between the various letters, using bold to increase emphasis. Yet some of the layouts are highly innovative (pp. XXXVIII-XXIX). In certain instances, slogans completely disrupt the conventional organisation of the printed page and the horizontal rhythm of the lines of type, normal to the book format. Occasionally, lines are broken up, and the slogans are presented at a dynamic diagonal. They seem to leap across the page. At the same time, the thick lines add emphasis and impact to crucial Constructivist slogans such as "Death to Art".[164]

Constructivism vividly evokes an industrial or machine aesthetic. With some justification, Gan later claimed that it had been one of the first examples of typographic design that had waged war on self-consciously "artistic" or "aesthetic" typography.[165] Although Gan had actually drawn the letters on the cover by hand,[166] presumably because the actual typeface he wanted was not available, his design was rooted in the typographical tools of the printing process. El Lissitzky later supported Gan's claims when he stated that Gan was the first person to begin working "directly in typography alongside the printer and with the machine".[167] Gan's emphasis on the technical process of mechanical reproduction is crucial to his concept of Constructivist graphic design. As Alexander Lavrentiev has explained, however, in the early 1920s there was a shortage of metal, so much of the type used was actually made of wood, just as some of the photographic and graphic material was reproduced from wood engravings made by Andrei Andreev.[168]

The principles and techniques that Gan had evolved in working on *Kino-Fot* and *Constructivism* were developed further in his later graphic work for magazines such as *Technology and Life* (*Tekhnika i zhizn'*)[169] and more especially in his work as the art editor for the journal *SA* for three years of its five-year existence (1926-1928). Gan developed a format for the cover of *SA*, which essentially remained unchanged from the second issue of 1926 until the third issue of 1929, despite minor alterations in the actual text used, and slight adjustments in the typeface and colours employed (pp. XLIV, XLVI-XLVII and back flap). The concept of variety within uniformity was clearly central to his approach and had characterised his work with *Kino-Fot*. In *SA*, he used it to great effect, rising to the challenge of making the grey drawings of plans and elevations visually interesting to the reader. He basically employed a grid format, using thick lines to create various frameworks around which and on which he organised the text (in various sizes and intensity of typefaces – some bold, others not) and images, employing asymmetrical organisation, spacing, and the white of the page as a positive factor in the design. In these ways, he created typographical layouts for the pages of *SA* which were exciting and dynamic, making the medium as effective as the message.

In 1925, Gan explained how the principles governing all Constructivist design could be applied to typography. He emphasised that the starting point for the design process was "the content of the text, its purpose and the points to be stressed".[170] At the same time, he highlighted the role that the tools of the printer and the production process of printing could play in the design. These included elements such as the actual type, the printing plate, lines and squares. He also underlined the significance of *faktura*, which in typography comprised the colour of the ink and the various qualities of the paper used. Above all, Gan stressed the overwhelming importance of the printing process as a determining factor for the designer. The covers of *SA* epitomise this approach – the format of the cover was produced by manipulating precisely those mechanically produced components about which he wrote, while subtle and dramatic changes were effected merely by changing the colour of the ink and the paper.

This approach not only epitomised the Constructivists' devotion to the machine, but also embodied their disdain for art itself and for the artist as a creative individual who was engaged on a qualitatively different kind of activity to that of other workers. Gan remained true to the concept of merging life and art, and asserted that his approach would also abolish the distinction between artist and worker. In 1925, he declared idealistically that "Through the book *Constructivism*, the issues of *Kino-Fot* and the posters for Goskino – we have tried to bring printed material to life again, and, most of all, to remind the workers about it. Show them that they could do it without the services of an art worker,

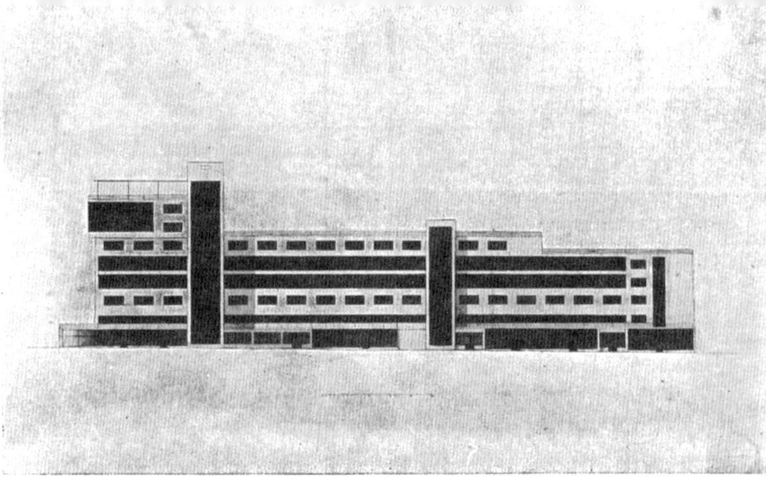

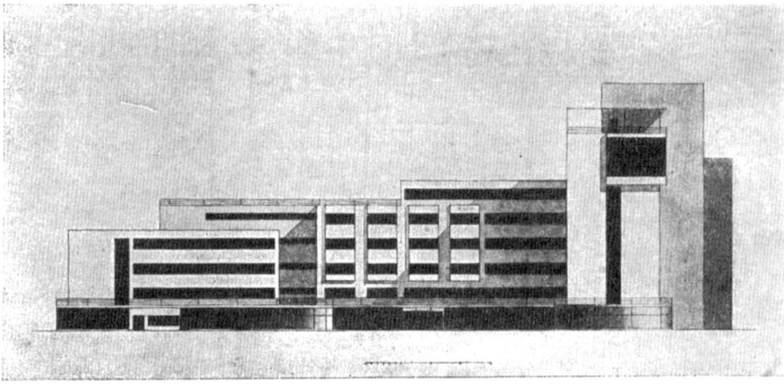

Л. А. и А. А. ВЕСНИНЫ. ПРОЕКТ „ДОМА ПРОМЫШЛЕННОСТИ И ТОРГОВЛИ" В Г. СВЕРДЛОВСКЕ, 1927. ЗДАНИЕ „ДОМА ПРОМЫШЛЕННОСТИ И ТОРГОВЛИ" ПРОЕКТИРУЕТСЯ НА УЧАСТКЕ, ВЫХОДЯЩЕМ НА ПЛОЩАДЬ ПАРИЖСКОЙ КОММУНЫ И УЛИЦУ ЛЕНИНА, С ОГРАНИЧИВАЮЩИМИ УЧАСТОК УЛИЦАМИ ВАСЕНЦОВСКОЙ И РЕШЕТНИКОВА.

ВВИДУ ОСОБОГО ЗНАЧЕНИЯ В ГОРОДСКОЙ ПЛАНИРОВКЕ ПЛОЩАДИ, НА КОТОРУЮ ВЫХОДЯТ ПРЕДПОЛАГАЕМЫЙ К ПОСТРОЙКЕ УРАЛОБЛИСПОЛКОМ И ГОРОДСКОЙ ТЕАТР, ГЛАВНЫЕ ФАСАДЫ ПРОЕКТИРУЕМОГО ЗДАНИЯ СО ВХОДАМИ В УЧРЕЖДЕНИЯ И МАГАЗИНЫ ОБРАЩЕНЫ НА ПЛОЩАДЬ И ПЕРЕСЕКАЮЩУЮ ЕЕ УЛ. ЛЕНИНА.

В ЦЕЛЯХ УВЕЛИЧЕНИЯ ПЕРИМЕТРА ВИТРИННОЙ ЛИНИИ МАГАЗИНОВ И ДЛЯ СОЗДАНИЯ УДОБНОГО ОСОБОГО ПОДЪЕЗДА В УРАЛОБЛСОВНАРХОЗ, НА ГЕНЕРАЛЬНОМ ПЛАНЕ В СТОРОНУ УЛИЦЫ ЛЕНИНА СПРОЕКТИРОВАН ОТКРЫТЫЙ ДВОР С ПЛОЩАДКОЙ ДЛЯ ГАЗОНА И МЕСТОМ ДЛЯ СТОЯНКИ АВТОМОБИЛЕЙ.

ЗДАНИЕ СО СТОРОНЫ ПЛОЩАДИ ОТСТУПАЕТ ОТ КРАСНОЙ ЛИНИИ НА ШИРИНУ АЛЛЕИ, ИДУЩЕЙ ВДОЛЬ ТРОТУАРА.

ЗДАНИЕ ПРОЕКТИРУЕТСЯ С ОДНИМ БОЛЬШИМ ВНУТРЕННИМ ДВОРОМ, ВОКРУГ КОТОРОГО ГРУППИРУЮТСЯ ВСЕ УЧРЕЖДЕНИЯ, ВХОДЯЩИЕ И СОСТАВЛЯЮЩИЕ „ДОМ ПРОМЫШЛЕННОСТИ И ТОРГОВЛИ". ПЕРИМЕТР ЗДАНИЯ ОБУСЛОВЛЕН СТРЕМЛЕНИЕМ ДАТЬ НАИБОЛЬШЕЕ ДНЕВНОЕ ОСВЕЩЕНИЕ КОРРИДОРАМ ПРИ ДВУХСТОРОННЕМ РАСПОЛОЖЕНИИ ПОМЕЩЕНИЙ.

КОРРИДОРЫ ИМЕЮТ ВСЮДУ ОСВЕЩЕНИЕ С ТОРЦОВ, С ЛЕСТНИЦ И ОСОБЫХ НИШ.

ЗДАНИЕ ПРОЕКТИРУЕТСЯ ЖЕЛЕЗОБЕТОННОЙ КОНСТРУКЦИИ С ЗАТЕПЛЕНИЕМ ПЛИТАМИ ТЕПЛОГО БЕТОНА В 40 *с* ТОЛЩИНЫ, КОТОРЫЕ СТАВЯТСЯ НА ЖЕЛЕЗОБЕТОННЫЕ ПРОГОНЫ УГЛОВОГО СЕЧЕНИЯ. НАРУЖНЫЙ РЯД ОКОННЫХ РАМ СТАВИТСЯ НА ЭТИ СТЕНКИ И НАХОДИТСЯ СНАРУЖИ КОЛОНН. ВНУТРЕННИЙ РЯД ОКОННЫХ РАМ ИДЕТ МЕЖДУ КОЛОННАМИ. ТАКАЯ КОНСТРУКЦИЯ СТЕНЫ ДОПУСКАЕТ ВОЗМОЖНОСТЬ УСТРОЙСТВА ЛЕГКИХ ПЕРЕДВИЖНЫХ ПЕРЕГОРОДОК, ИДУЩИХ ДО ВНУТРЕННИХ РАМ.

КОЛОННЫ ПО НАРУЖНОМУ ПЕРИМЕТРУ РАССТАВЛЕНЫ НА 6,8 *м* МЕЖДУ ОСЯМИ, ГЛУБИНА ПОМЕЩЕНИЙ ВЗЯТА 6 *м*, ШИРИНА КОРРИДОРОВ—3 *м*.

ТАКОЕ РАСПОЛОЖЕНИЕ КОЛОНН ДАЛО СТАНДАРТНЫЙ РАЗМЕР ПОМЕЩЕНИЙ В 40,08 $м^2$, КОТОРЫЙ ЛЕГКО ДЕЛИТСЯ ДЛЯ ПОЛУЧЕНИЯ ВСТРЕЧАЮЩИХСЯ В ПРОГРАММЕ ПЛОЩАДЕЙ В 40 $м^2$, 60 $м^2$, 30 $м^2$, 20 $м^2$ И Т. Д.

РАБОЧАЯ ПЛОЩАДЬ В ПОМЕЩЕНИЯХ ПРИНЯТА В 3,7 m^2 НА ОДНОГО СОТРУДНИКА.

ВЫСОТА ЭТАЖЕЙ С КОНСТРУКЦИЕЙ — 4,25 *м*. ОБЩАЯ КУБАТУРА ЗДАНИЯ—ОКОЛО 160000 $м^3$..

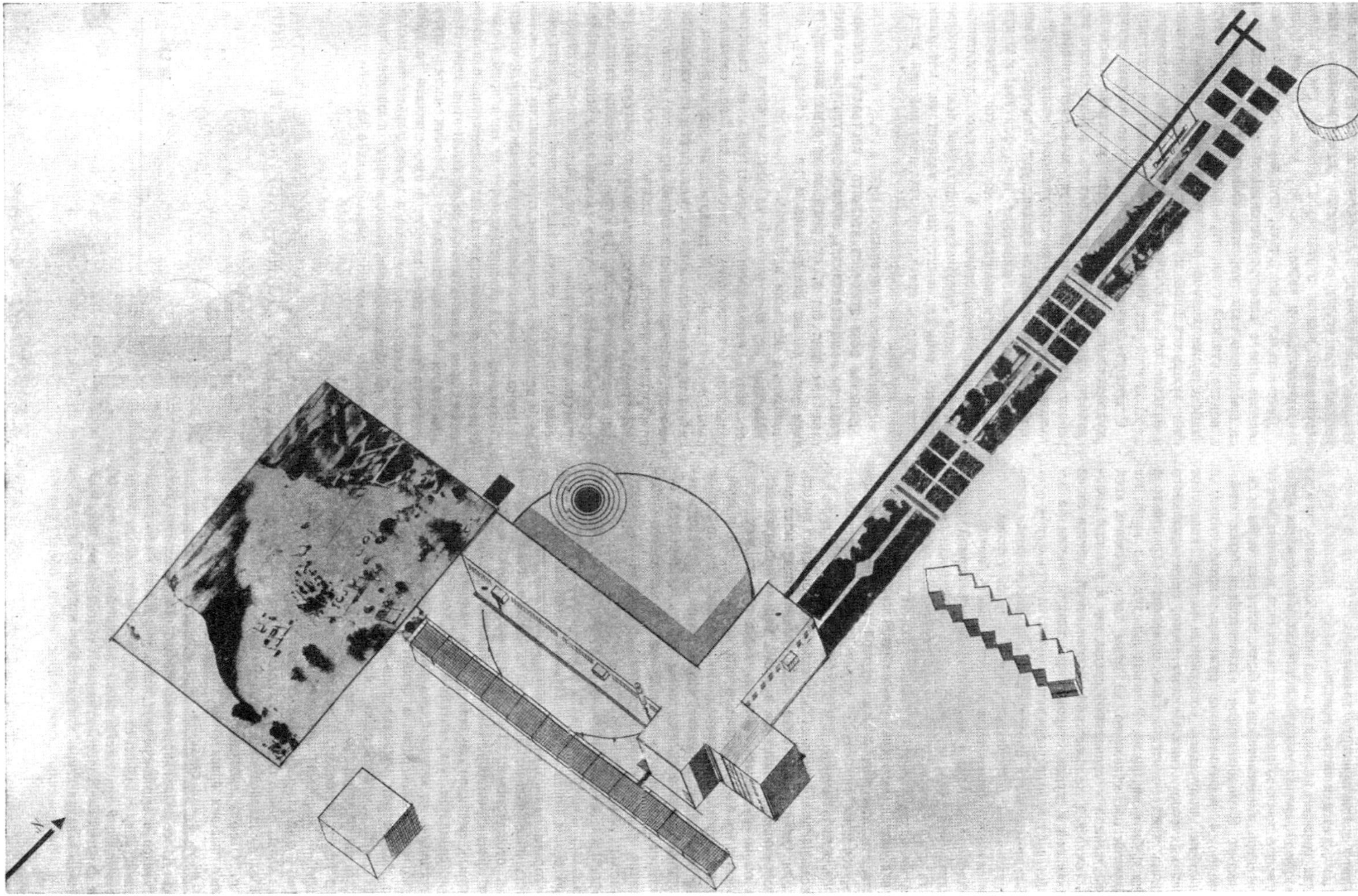

И. ЛЕОНИДОВ. КОНКУРСНЫЙ ПРОЕКТ КИНО-ФАБРИКИ. 1927. МЕСТО РАСПОЛОЖЕНИЯ—ВОРОБЬЕВЫ ГОРЫ. АКСОНОМЕТРИЯ. СОСТАВ: АТЕЛЬЕ, ПРАВЛЕНИЕ, ГАРАЖ, МАСТЕРСКИЕ, УМФОРМЕРНАЯ ПОДСТАНЦИЯ. j. LEONIDOFF. ENTWURF FÜR EIN KINO-ATELIER. 1927. AXONMETRISCHE DARSTELLUNG.

СКЛАДНОЙ СТАНОК МОССЕЛЬПРОМ

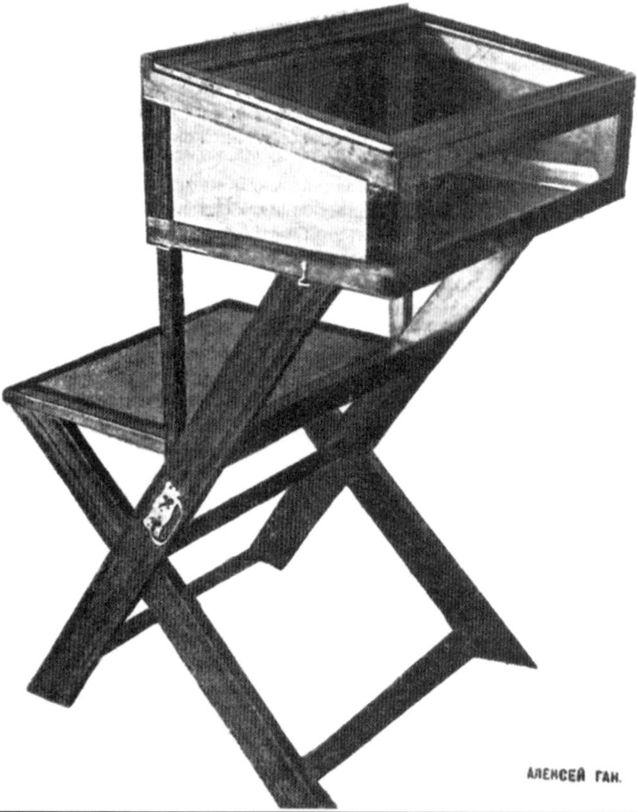

АЛЕКСЕЙ ГАН.

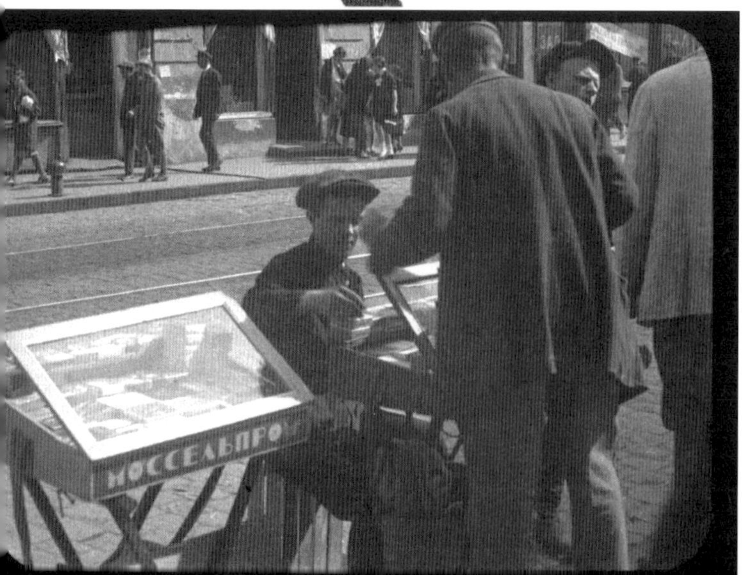

and push them along the path of [taking] production initiatives."[171] The implication of this statement is that any working person is capable of manipulating the production tools of the typographer without any specialised training, and that they, too, could produce Constructivist typographical designs. This sentiment, of course, echoes those utopian ideas that were ultimately related to the concepts of Marx's *German Ideology*, a text which was only partially known at this time, but which envisaged a society in which every person's potential would be realised, and the distinctions between artists and non-artists would vanish.

Gan as an Industrial Designer

In *Constructivism*, Gan had written extensively about architecture, but as far as we know, he never designed any actual buildings. The closest he came to such activity was in his designs for a few kiosks, which were mainly temporary structures. Yet in these he was exploring one of the tasks that he had set Constructivism, which was "To create a system for the design of objects in general."[172]

Amongst the earliest was his Folding Sales Stand (*skladnoi stanok*, p.LX) of 1922, produced for Mossel'prom (*Moskovskoe obedinenie predpriatiya po pererabotke produktov sel'sko-khozyaistvennoi promyshlennosti* – Moscow Association of Businesses for Processing Products of the Agricultural Industry).[173] Gan devised a small folding structure, apparently made from wood, which could be carried to its destination and then quickly erected in the street or any open public space. After use, it could easily be re-folded and carried away. It contained a tray (on collapsible legs) with a removable glass lid for displaying small items of merchandise such as stationary supplies or cigarettes. It also incorporated a small seat on which the seller could sit while waiting for customers. With a few minor alterations, sales stands based on this idea seem to have been produced during the 1920s and were photographed by Rodchenko. When he published this piece in *SA* in 1926, Gan stressed that "Constructivism must direct its attention towards this [i.e. street furniture] and take responsibility for the everyday life of the street".[174]

Gan also designed a larger structure for the sale of books, stationary items, paper and journals in about 1923 for Vserokompom (*Vserossiiskii komitet pomoshchi invalidam voiny* – All Russian Committee for Help to War Invalids,p. LXII).[175] This was not a portable piece in the sense that it could be easily carried around by one person, but it could be moved. It consisted essentially of two cuboid

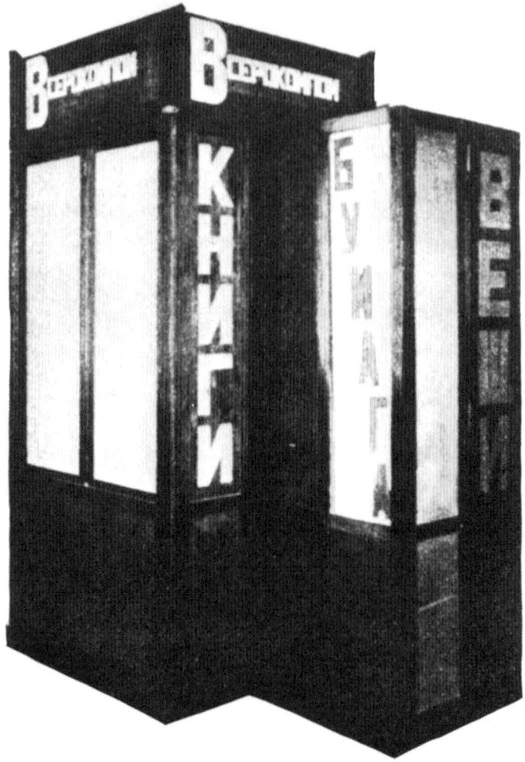
ВСЕРОКОМПОМ
ВСЕРОКОМПОМ
КНИГИ

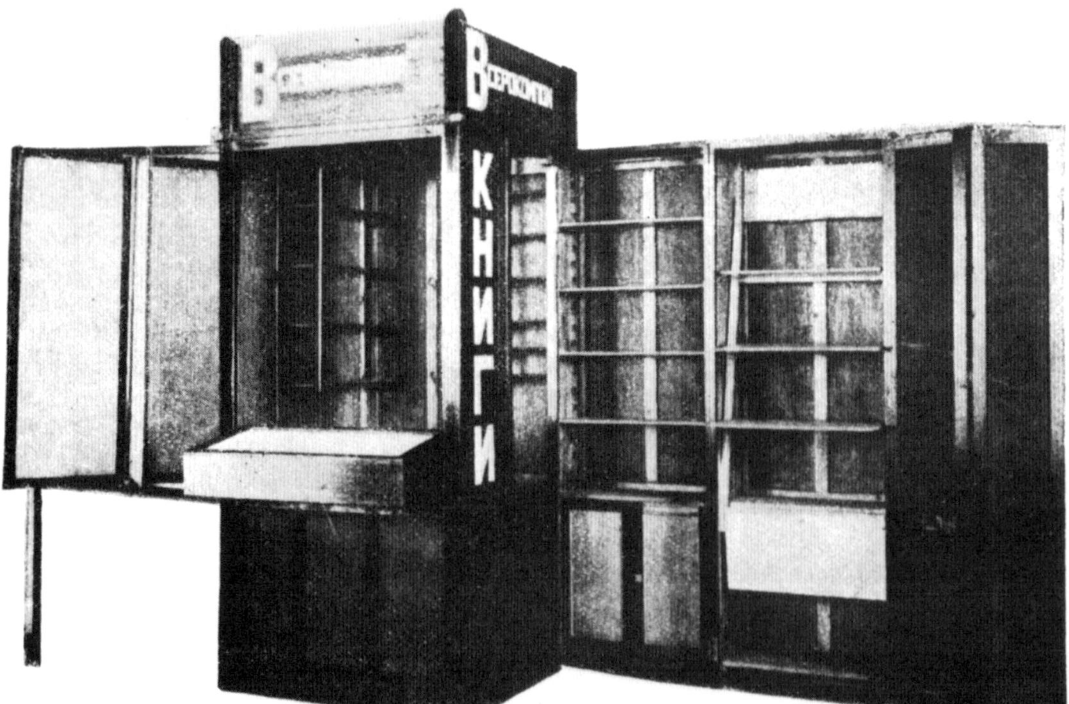
ВСЕРОКОМПОМ
КНИГИ

structures of different sizes, which together opened out to create a large area of shelving for displaying books and magazines. This prototype clearly went into production at some point and, with certain modifications, was manufactured from wood, for use inside public buildings, like the entrance halls of Moscow metro stations, where some examples were still in use until very recently. When shut, the contents were secure, although the prominent lettering advertised the items on sale (books, stationary items and paper), announced the role of the kiosk and with the coloured panels provided elements of decoration.

A more adventurous approach to geometry characterised Gan's design for a Rural Kiosk (p. LXVI), which was commissioned by *The Peasant Newspaper* (*Krest'yanskaya gazeta*) in 1925.[176] Primarily intended for the sale of books, it was also expected to serve as a focal point for the village's social activities. Formally, the design possesses affinities with the sketches of kiosks that Rodchenko himself had made in 1919, using an expressive combination of coloured geometric elements,[177] although Gan's geometry is more precise and the structure more coherent. In the rural kiosk, the white walls seem to reflect elements of the International Style in Europe, about which Gan would have learnt from journals like *L'Esprit Nouveau* and *Object*, with which he was clearly familiar since he mentioned them in *Constructivism* and had reprinted articles from them in *Kino-Fot*.[178]

Ideological considerations were clearly an important factor in the conception of the design. The expressive exterior was intended to perform a political function and reinforce the kiosk's role as a centre for disseminating the communist message. Visually, the kiosk looked like a piece of urban architecture in a rural setting – a discordant but also a provocative and arresting element. As a distinctive building, which was very different to the surrounding structures, it would stand out as much as the church, which had previously been the most prominent architectural structure in the village and the source of those religious values that had hitherto dominated peasant life. The kiosk had to be visible from all points in the village.[179] Similarly the kiosk's modernity emphasised the new values of communism. In this way, Gan's design acted as a piece of visual propaganda contributing to the "sovietisation of the countryside" and functioned as a "cultural link between the city and the village".[180] In an attempt to convey structurally the important ideological role that the kiosk was to play in the life of the community, Gan turned his design into a piece of permanent propaganda and made it literally look like a flag ship. The nautical imagery was utilised in the prow-like arrangement of the façade and the rigging, with structures echoing the crows' nest, and the funnels being attached to the roof.

ДЕРЕВЕНСКИЙ КИОСК

Проект — макет

Конструктивист Алексей Ган

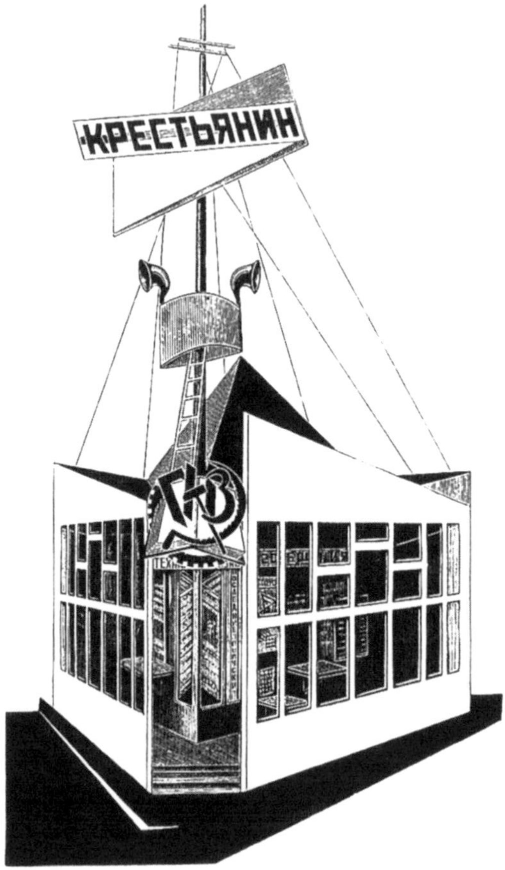

Советизация деревни идет различными путями. Трактор и электрификация, кооперирование сельского населения, новые способы культурной обработки земли, политико-просветительная работа и многое другое — все в целом — составляет ту колоссальную социально-культурную деятельность, которую развивает в деревне Советская власть, партия и пролетарская общественность.

Вовлеченные в строительство новых общественных и хозяйственных форм крестьяне — в силу недостатка средств — продолжают пребывать в старых условиях домашнего быта двора-избы, и даже их общественные очаги, которые становятся уже неотъемлемой частью со етской деревни (избы-читальни, клубы и прочее) так же остаются архитектурно неоформленными.

В деревнях - селах попрежнему только церковь является, так сказать, архитектурным местом. Ей нет соперника здания в деревне, которое бы своим пребыванием в архитектурной среде сельских строений агитировало за новый быт деревни.

Учитывая наше экономическое положение и понимая, что в данное время трудно подойти к практическому осуществлению постройки новых зданий даже для общественных нужд деревни, хочется хотя бы в самых скромных размерах подойти к этой задаче вне очереди.

Настоящими соображениями и руководствовался автор проекта.

Киоск сконструирован так.

В смысле функционального назначения в нем должны увязаться две формы деятельности: торговая и общественная. Торговая — по сбыту литературы, писчебумажных материалов и принадлежностей; общественная — по обслуживанию местного населения культурной связью деревни с городом, через почту, радио и кино-экран. Кроме того, киоск должен стать центральным местом для массовых форм рабоче-крестьянской общественности.

Внешний вид его представляет из себя треугольник (план) со срезанными углами и скошенными фасадными плоскостями. Треугольник вызван теми обстоятельствами, что улицы деревни в большинстве не организованы, а установка его не должна рассчитывать на особое для себя планирование местности.

Сооружение же должно быть в одинаковой мере видно со всех точек зрения полно и равно.

Трех-ярусное построение по вертикали и трех-линейное разделение самого плана по горизонтали, также вызваны рабочими функциями киоска.

Фасадные плоскости срезаны для того, чтобы сток воды и сползание снега происходило в трех направлениях, а не в шести. Это дало возможность расширить кубатуру второго яруса и использовать ее под помещение для товара.

Материальное оформление — дерево, листовое железо и стекло.

Андрей Новиков.

Although these nautical features make the Rural Kiosk visually arresting and architecturally exciting, reference to shipping might seem somewhat inappropriate for the rural setting of the vast land-locked areas of Russia. Of course, contemporary liners had become paradigms of efficiency for architects like Le Corbusier, and Gan may have been evoking the achievements of contemporary architecture and engineering in this way. He may, however, have also been imbuing his design with a more specific revolutionary connotation by alluding to the battleship Aurora, which had given the signal that had launched the Bolshevik attack on the Winter Palace on 25 October 1917. The battleship had summoned the populace of Petrograd to revolution. Presumably Gan hoped that the rural reading room would summon the local people to imbibe the revolutionary message, and that it would act as a focal point for engendering and promoting the revolution in the countryside.

In other respects, Gan's design displays an admirable pragmatism. It was to be made of wood, glass and sheet metal and divided up vertically and horizontally to provide spaces for the building's various functions. The ground plan was triangular since most villages were not built on a regular grid pattern and so a triangular format would be more adaptable and more easily fitted in to available sites. The steep inclines of the walls and roofs were justified on climatic grounds: it was intended to channel the snow and rain in such a way as to keep the entrance clear. Despite this, the whole design has a decidedly more rhetorical feel than Gan's more temporary structures such as the folding sales stand and his book kiosk, and, of course, there is no evidence whatsoever that it was ever manufactured. For Gan, the design and production of such items was important evidence that "Constructivism has not only theoretically solved the problem of rationalising artistic work, but is indeed already putting into practice its new forms and participating in the building of the material culture of the present".[181]

Gan and Constructivist Cinema

As well as being interested in the theory and practice of film-making and publishing the latest achievements in these areas, alongside information about specific films, their content and techniques in *Kino-Fot, Long Live the Demonstration of Life!*, and various articles, Gan also made four films between 1924 and 1925: *Island of the Young Pioneers* (*Ostrov yunykh pionerov*); *The Seventh October* (*Sed'moi Oktyabr'*); *Trades Unions* (*Treid-yunionyi*); and *Greetings*

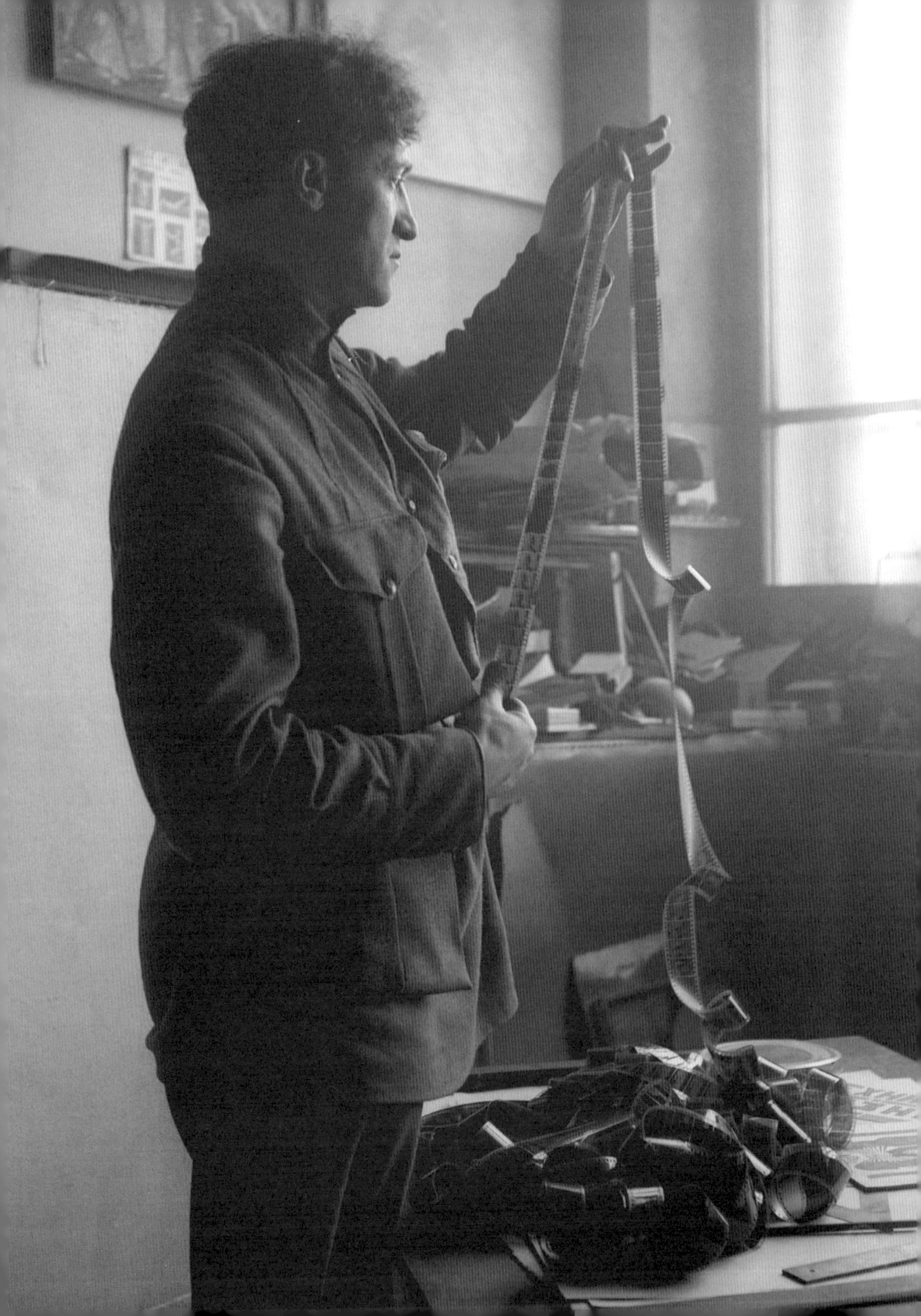

Teamworkers (*Privet, kadrony*). None of these were great successes and none have survived as full length features. Nevertheless some frames from *The Island of the Young Pioneers* can be found in the archives of Gosfilm (State Film Company), and a few stills are also known since they were reproduced as illustrations for the film's reviews.

The Island of the Young Pioneers was ostensibly a documentary. The initial impulse for its shooting seems to have been a campaign to attract more working-class youngsters to film making, which was orchestrated by the Society of the Builders of Proletarian Cinema (*Obshchestvo stroitel'ei proletarskogo kino* – OSPK), itself organised by Proletkino (*Proletarskoe kino* – Proletarian cinema).[182] From 1918 onwards Gan had consistently argued for a proletarian theatre made by proletarians, so would naturally have endorsed a campaign to promote the making of proletarian films by proletarians. In *Kino-Fot* and elsewhere Gan had also stated his opposition to the acted film as opposed to the documentary. He asserted, "The decorator, actor and director are not needed in cinema; and furthermore! They are harmful to its development".[183] He elaborated this standpoint in *Long Live the Demonstration of Life!*, which dealt at length with the work of Vertov. In this text, Gan argued that real life presented the most valuable subject for the film-maker and he stressed that "above all it is essential to learn how to capture everyday life".[184] He elaborated:

> One would have to be blind not to notice how everyday life is developing dialectically, growing from the new industrial and social relationships. It is essential to be able to discern the fluidity of its forms and understand that it is arising directly from the whole complexity of rapidly changing political moments and once again developing from the economic conditions of economic decline or renewal. Then it will become clear that everyday life as an object-based and material form of human society ... will stabilise and be preserved, will become immobile, and, then, on the contrary in the stormy period of revolutionary reconstruction will be transformed ... This is the vital and real strength of everyday life at a time when its revolutionary content is becoming less intense in the smooth, outwardly effective, formal and material work of the active, living masses – only film can capture this successfully and through montage convey it on the screens of a mass auditorium.[185]

This description corresponds to what we know about the views on cinema that Gan had expressed in *Kino-Fot* – the need to capture life in its revolutionary

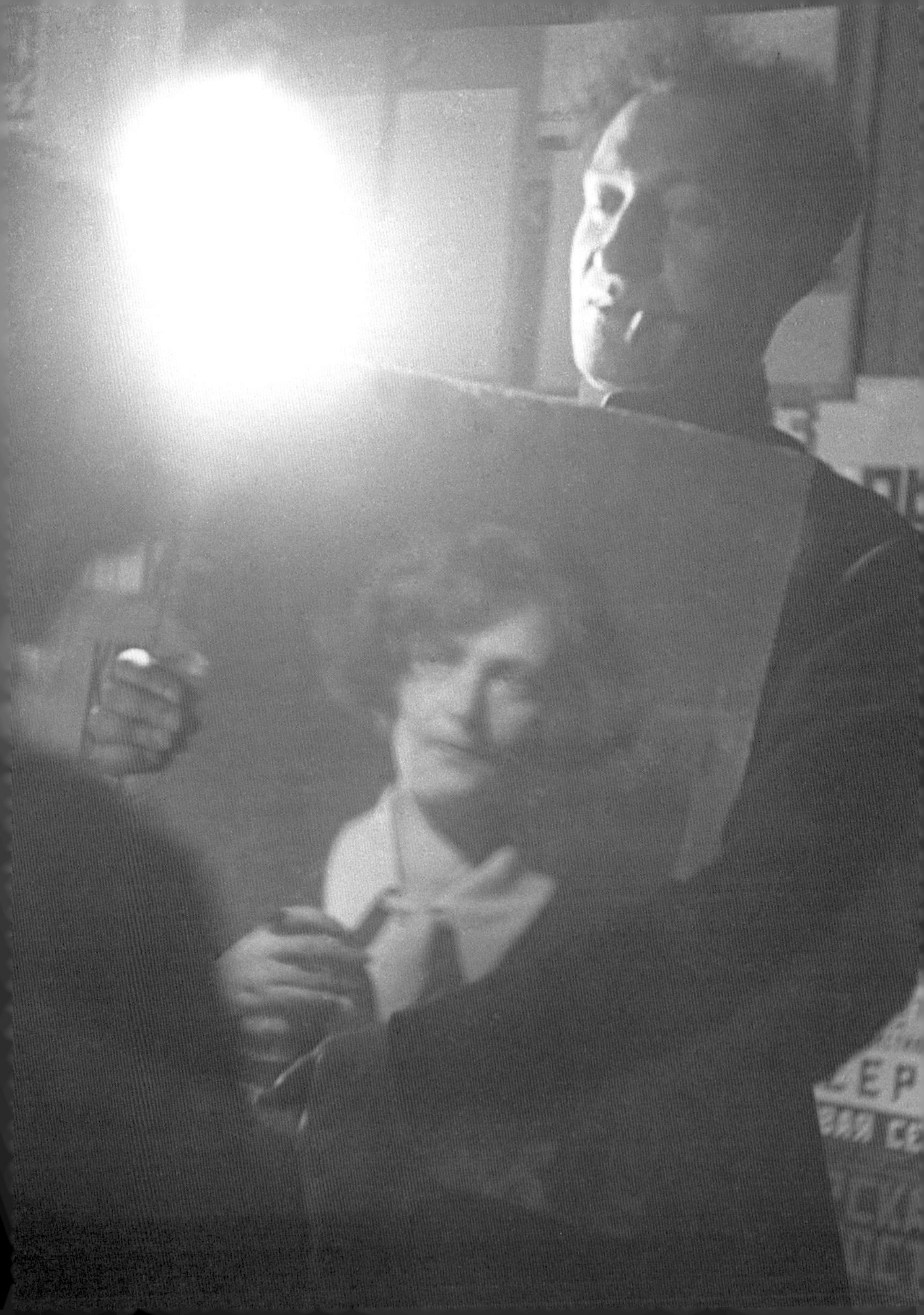

transformation and assist that transformation. Yet *Long Live the Demonstration of Life!* also contains a poetic evocation of human relationships and emotions, which unexpectedly reveals Gan's own humanity:

> To observe carefully life's most varied aspects, as if encountering unfamiliar forms of phenomena at every step, an endless string of new expressions of life, which individually or collectively the citizens of the Soviet Republic actually allow. Studying their movements, listening to their conversations, detecting connections, discerning relationships, you begin to understand this energetic, incessant stream of people as a continuously moving form with a constantly evolving content. In this bustling and unrestrained exterior, it is impossible not to detect a functional content that hits one in the eyes, and the essence of which appears where material conditions clash with human desires and will.[186]

It was probably with the aspiration to capture this flow of human relationships and inter-action that Gan embarked on shooting *The Island of the Young Pioneers* with financial support from Vertov.[187] Mikhail Vladimirskii was the cameraman, and the film was shot in an actual pioneer camp (for pioneers from the Bauman district of Moscow) on the banks of the Moscow River in the region of Zvenigorod.[188] Gan was director and Esfir Shub was the editor.[189]

The film caused a scandal because it wasn't a documentary, but an acted film, despite all Gan's theorising and protestations that "there is not a whiff in any of my work of professional acting".[190] In fact, Gan used a script, written by Vladimir Verevkin, and, although they were not professional actors, the pioneers did act out the film's narrative story line, about two children who reject their father's drinking and take strength from the pioneer collective and eventually manage to reform him. Not surprisingly, the film produced some virulent attacks on Gan, some highly negative reviews and led to a split with Vertov, who harshly criticised his former colleague and friend.[191]

Dissension has also characterised scholarly evaluations of the film. Romberg considers that Gan was trying to reconcile the stark division between fiction and documentary, using the script as a stimulus for action rather than an imposed straightjacket, and thus attempting to fuse aspects of art and life into a new approach. In contrast, Lavrentiev dismisses the film as clumsy and inartistic, declaring that "Vertov was an artist. Gan was a sociologist".[192]

Despite the attacks and discouragements, Gan did not totally relinquish his interest in film and the cinema. In 1926 he was campaigning for an institute devoted to the newsreel. He proposed that such an establishment would collect copies of all newsreels made in the Soviet Union and would provide the same kind of support and favourable conditions for film-makers concerned with making documentaries and newsreels as for those engaged on shooting commercial films.[193]

Keeping the Constructivist Flame Alive

Gan was concerned to keep the flame of pure Constructivism alive and was committed to the original notion of Constructivism as he had enunciated it in the "Programme of the Working Group of Constructivists" in March 1921. As an aspect of this strategy, he emphasised the distinction between Constructivism in the Soviet Union and Western Europe. In *Constructivism*, he asserted that the Berlin journal *Veshch'/Gegenstand/Objet*, published by El Lissitzky and Ilya Ehrenburg in two issues in Spring 1922 (Nos. 1-2, and 3) belonged exclusively to Western Constructivism, and he was at pains to disassociate it from Soviet Constructivism.[194] He stressed, "The fundamental mistake of comrades Erenburg and Lissitzky is that they cannot tear themselves away from art. They simply call the new art Constructivism".[195] Gan's criticism of *Object* as not Constructivist was clearly shared by other theorists, such as Boris Arvatov.[196] Yet Gan's hostility may not have been merely theoretical; it might have been reinforced by tactical considerations. Gan may have wanted to preserve Soviet Constructivism from any taint of being involved with the emigration, especially in the early 1920s, when avant-garde creative figures had lost their positions of influence in the government and official support for them was disappearing. Moreover, the regime was beginning to promote realism, and the New Economic Policy (which allowed small-scale free enterprise to coexist with state run heavy industry) was leading to the re-emergence of an entrepreneurial class with philistine cultural values.

Gan's intransigence, his rigorous commitment to communism, his extremist anti-art stance and adamant opposition to any hint of stylisation or aesthetics in the design process was probably the reason for the various divisions that seem to have plagued the history of Constructivism in the Soviet Union itself. In January 1922, the Stenberg brothers and Medunetskii had held their own exhibition, effectively asserting their independence from the rest of the group and their own identity as Constructivists.[197] In response to this event, Gan added "First" to the group's name in order to distinguish himself, Rodchenko and Stepanova from these younger artists.[198]

Probably because of his publications, notably *Kino-Fot* and *Constructivism*, Gan was an influential figure in early 1923. In February, the artist Nikolai Kupreyanov observed that "Moscow is really inhabited chiefly by Sidorovites [followers of the conservative art critic Aleksei Sidorov] and to a lesser extent Ganites [followers of Gan]."[199]

In 1924 Gan seems to have been involved in some kind of creative split with Stepanova and Rodchenko.[200] At the *First Discussional Exhibition of Associations of Active Revolutionary Art* in 1924, The First Working Group of Constructivists no longer included them, but was presented as comprising Gan himself and a small group of acolytes: Georgii Miller, L. Sanina, Aleksandra Mirolyubova, and the sisters Galina and Olga Chichagova. In the catalogue, Gan explained, "Constructivists, not in word, but in actuality, bring into existence an object of real value, improving its quality, and establishing its social role, and organising its form in an organic relationship with its utilitarian significance and purpose."[201]

The split was evidently not personal as Rodchenko, Stepanova and Gan continued to be friends. In 1925, Rodchenko wrote to Stepanova from Paris:

> Tell Alyosha [Gan] that our masters [Vertov et al] aren't recognised abroad, only their own or those who have always lived here [Westerners or permanent residents]; that they'll filch everything good ... I regret a thousand times over that I gave work to the exhibition ...
> And we have to keep together and build a new relationship between workers in art labour. We can't organise any everyday life if our own relationships resemble the relationships of bohemians in the West. That's the problem. First – is our everyday life. Second – is to choose well and hold tightly together and believe in one another ...
> Alyosha is an individualist, and, like Tatlin, he's begun thinking that he's the [only] pure Constructivist.[202]

After receiving vitriolic reviews for *The Island of the Young Pioneers*, and having failed to secure a showing of the film in the West, Gan seems to have decided to give up film-making, prompting Rodchenko, who was in Paris to write in June 1925, "What! Has Alyosha given up the cinema?"[203] Rodchenko had evidently been supportive of Gan's activity in this sphere and had displayed his friend's poster for the film on the walls of his Workers' Club at the 1925 Paris exhibition.[204] At this point, Gan seems to have been having substantial problems. On 16 May 1925, Stepanova wrote to Rodchenko:

> Yesterday there was another difficult scene with Alyosha. It's hard to describe in detail, but the main idea was that we have forgotten him and he feels persecuted. He's jealous of [Vitalii] Zhemchuzhnyi He was a little drunk and even cried. But still. I'd like you to write him a friendly letter. Well, I think you'll understand yourself that his situation is difficult.[205]

Undoubtedly, Gan was at his most energetic and committed, and expressed his most radical ideas in the first half of the 1920s, when he was still enthused by the vision of a new kind of life in the Soviet Union and sustained by a belief that it could actually be realised. By 1925, he was less confident, and beginning to recognise that the revolution of which he dreamed was no longer feasible. He wrote to his wife that the present was "incredibly complicated":

> On the one hand, we are making progress, i.e. our economy is recovering, but on the other, we must go back to elementary reading books, to pictures, to spectacles, to film dramas, etc. etc. For me, this means either embracing this work and rejecting everything that I have worked on all these years, or not abandoning my production (typography, cinema, and structures, above all), and now occupying myself exclusively with great scientific and theoretical work. The time for slogans ... has passed in general, and for me *in particular*.[206]

Despite periods in psychiatric hospitals during the later 1920s, Gan continued to be active and was even involved in the organisation of the October Group, which represents one of the final positions adopted by avant-garde artists who were associated with Constructivism.[207] The October group was an attempt to unite innovative creative figures against the government-sponsored realist groups in art and literature, especially the aggressive realist artists of the Association of Artists of the Revolution (*Assotsiatsiya khudozhnikov revolyutsii* – AKhR). Like the "Programme of the Working Group of Constructivists", October's declaration explicitly embraced the Bolshevik Revolution, while emphasising the role of design in achieving communism, but also allowing a role for pure art in this trajectory. Hence, it declared that an artist is "an active fighter at the ideological front of the Proletarian Revolution" who must "create new types and a new style of the spatial arts", "design materially the mass, collective forms of the new life", and "organise the consciousness, will and emotions of the proletariat and the working masses with maximum force". It advocated the "organic cooperation of spatial art forms", emphasised the importance of the industrial arts and the need for an "art of the masses". It also indicated five areas of activity:

architecture and the rational construction of new buildings; the artistic design of objects for mass production; the artistic design of centres such as workers' clubs for the new, collective way of life; the organisation of mass festivals; and art education. In addition, it contested the validity of any one creative group to dominance, which it acknowledged was "a radical contradiction of the Party's and government's artistic policy" which promoted AKhR and similar groupings. Figures like Gustavs Klucis, Aleksandr Vesnin and Aleksandr Rodchenko all signed up. But the writing was on the wall, and official preferences for traditional artistic approaches ensured that this organisation was short-lived.

As an active presence, Gan seems to have disappeared from avant-garde view towards the end of 1928, just after he was admitted to hospital. Nevertheless, his name continued to feature on the editorial board of *SA*, and his design format for the cover remained, although from the fourth issue of 1929 onwards, the design changed quite frequently. Similarly, the pages inside continued to use Gan's typographical emphasis on the thick line, but it was frequently employed to less dramatic effect.

Gan the man may have disappeared from view, but his contribution remained. Gan not only gave an articulate form to the ideas of the Constructivists, he also extended and developed the theories behind Constructivist practice. It was Gan who first put forward the notion of Constructivist photography in 1922. It was Gan who forged a relationship between Constructivism and the cinema. It was Gan who also took the first steps in evolving the theory and practice of Constructivist typography. It was Gan who first emphasised the need for a new architecture. In addition to this, although largely unrecognized, Gan was, to a certain extent, an innovative designer in his own right, particularly in the fields of kiosk and graphic design. Gan is one of the unsung heroes of Constructivism. As Stepanova observed, "It is not such an easy matter to conduct agitation for Constructivism and it is even more difficult to reject art and to begin to work in production."[208] Gan embraced these difficulties enthusiastically. He created the theory of Constructivism, agitated for Constructivism and he tried to implement Constructivism in his typography, design and film work, indefatigably promoting and publicising the principles in which he believed so firmly, and which he was convinced would ultimately lead to a better world and help to produce a communist society.

NOTES ON THE INTRODUCTION

1. For the first brief biographies and study of Gan's work, see Szymon Bojko, *New Graphic Design in Revolutionary Russia* (New York and Washington: Praeger Publishers, 1972), p. 146; John E. Bowlt, ed., and trans., *Russian Art of the Avant-Garde: Theory and Criticism 1902-1934* (New York: The Viking Press, 1976), pp. 214-217; and Christina Lodder, *Russian Constructivism* (New Haven and London: Yale University Press, 1983), pp. 98-99 and 243-244.

2. See, for instance, Aleksandr Lavrent'ev, "Zagadka Alekseya Gana", *Da!*, no. 2-3 (1995), pp. 3-10; and Catherine Cooke, "Sources of a Radical Mission in the Early Soviet Profession: Aleksei Gan and the Moscow Anarchists", in Neil Leach, ed., *Architecture and Revolution: Contemporary Perspectives on Central and Eastern Europe* (London and New York: Routledge, 1999), pp. 13-37.

3. A. N. Lavrent'ev, *Aleksei Gan* (Moscow: S. E. Gordeev, 2010).

4. Kristin Romberg, "Labor Demonstrations: Aleksei Gan's *Island of the Young Pioneers*, Dziga Vertov's *Kino-Eye*, and the Rationalization of Artistic Labor", *October* (New York) no. 145 (summer 2013), p. 38-66; Kristin Romberg, "Tektonika", in Sergei Ushakin, ed., *Formy i struktury. Antologiya rossiiskogo modernizma* (Moscow: Kabinetnyi uchenyi, 2013; Kristin Romberg "Aleksei Gan's Constructivism 1918-1928" (Ph.D., University of Columbia, New York, 2010); and her forthcoming book on Gan.

5. See Lodder, *Russian Constructivism*; and S. O. Khan-Magomedov, *Vhutemas: Moscou 1920-1930* (Paris: Éditions du Regard, 1990).

6. Varvara Stepanova, *Chelovek ne mozhet zhit' bez chuda. Pis'ma. Poeticheskie opyty. Zapiski khudozhnitsy*, ed. O. V. Mel'nikov (Moscow: Izdatel'stvo Sfera, 1994), p. 108.

7. For Gan's biographical details, see Romberg, "Aleksei Gan's Constructivism".

8. Romberg, "Tektonika".

9. See A. I. Konopleva, "Aleksei Mikhailovich Gan", *Kinovedcheskie zapiski* (Moscow), no. 49 (2006), pp. 212-221.

10. Romberg, "Tektonika".

11. Stepanova, *Chelovek*, p. 104.

12. For their relationship, see V. V. Zabrodina, "'... Bolezn' moya innogo poryadka'. Pis'ma Alekseya Gana Esfiri Shub", *Kinovedcheskie zapiski*, no. 49 (2006), pp. 222-228; and V. V. Zabrodina "Pis'mo Esfiri Shub Alekseyu Ganu", *Kinovedcheskie zapiski*, no. 49 (2006), pp. 229-230.

13. Konopleva, "Aleksei Mikhailovich Gan".

14. Konopleva, "Aleksei Mikhailovich Gan".

15. Viktor Vesnin, cited in Zabrodina, "'... Bolezn' moya innogo poryadka'", pp. 229.

16. Stepanova, *Chelovek*, p. 66.

17. Lavrent'ev, *Aleksei Gan*, p. 79.

Revolutionary Theatre

18. A. Gan, "Togda, teper' i my", *Anarkhiya* (Moscow), (26 April 1918).

19. Romberg, "Tektonika".

20. A. Gan, "Togda, teper' i my".

21. A.A Gvozdaev and ADR. Piotrovskii "Petrogradskie teatry i prazdnestva v epokhu voennogo kommunizma" in V. E. Rafalovich, ed., *Istoria sovetskogo teatra* (Leningrad, 1933), p. 262.

22. For a history of Proletkult, see Lynn Mally, *Culture of the Future: The Proletkult Movement in Revolutionary Russia* (Berkeley, Los Angeles and Oxford: University of California Press, 1990). Mally does not mention Gan.

23. See Aleksei Gan, "Bor'ba za 'Massovoe Deistvo'" in I. Aksenov, B Arvatov, E. Beskin, V. Blyum, A. Gan, O. Blyum, M. Zagorskii, V. Rappoport, L Sabaneev, V. Tikhonovich and B. Ferdinandov, *O teatre* (Tver', 1922), p. 51. Gan gives the date as 28 December 1920.

24. Cited in E. Sidorina, "Liki konstruktivizma", *Iskusstvoznanie* (Moscow), vol. 1, no. 2 (2007), p. 477.

25. "Vozzvanie sektsii massovykh predstavleni i zrelishch", *Vestnik teatra* (Moscow), no. 50 (1920), p. 2.

26. See Konstantin Rudnitsky, *Russian and Soviet Theatre: Tradition and the Avant-Garde*, trans. Roxane Permar, ed. Lesley Milne (London: Thames and Hudson, 1988), p. 60.

27. A. Gan, "Nasha bor'ba", *Vestnik teatra*, no. 75-77 (29 November 1920), p. 6.

28. Stepanova, *Chelovek*, p. 147. Rodchenko listed thirteen of these costume designs for display at the *Exposition Internationale des Arts Décoratifs et Industriels Modernes*, Paris, 1925. See *Aleksandr Rodchenko: Experiments for the Future: Diaries, Essays, Letters and Other Writings*, ed. Alexander Lavrentiev, trans. Jamey Gambrell (New York: The Museum of Modern Art, 2005), p. 149.

29. *Aleksandr Rodchenko: Experiments for the Future*, p. 128.

30. *Aleksandr Rodchenko: Experiments for the Future*, p. 128.

31. Lavrent'ev, *Aleksei Gan*, p. 60. Nevertheless, Rodchenko's list of costumes for the 1925 Paris exhibition, included the words "*We*, text by Aleksei Gan", implying that a libretto did exist (*Aleksandr Rodchenko: Experiments for the Future*, p. 149).

32. See "Plan organizatsii pervomaiskikh torzhestv na ulitsakh Moskvy, razrabotannyi sektsiei massovykh predstavleni I zrelishch teatral'nogo otdela Narkomprosa", *Vestnik teatra*, no. 51 (5-8 February 1920), pp. 6-8; English translation in Vladimir Tolstoy, Irina Bibikova and Catherine Cooke, eds., *Street Art of the Revolution: Festivals and Celebrations in Russia 1918-33*, trans. Frances Longman and Vladimir Vnukov (London: Thames and Hudson, 1990), pp. 124-6.

33. "Plan organizatsii", *Street Art*, p. 12.

34. See "Soobshcheniya ob organizatsii prazdnovaniya 1 Maya 1920 v Moskve", *Vestnik teatra*, no. 62 (27 April - 2 May 1920), p. 13; *Street Art*, 126.

35. "Plan organizatsii", *Street Art*, p. 125.

36. See Catherine Cooke, *Russian Avant-Garde: Theories of Art, Architecture and the City* (London: Academy Editions, 1995), pp. 23-24.

37. For a full description of this mass action and an indication of its importance for the subsequent development of Constructivist design, see Christina Lodder, "Lyubov Popova: A Revolutionary Woman Artist" in Christina Lodder, *Constructive Strands in Russian Art 1914-1937* (London: Pindar Press, 2005), pp. 426-458, especially pp. 428ff.

Forging Links with Avant-Garde Artists

38. Lavrent'ev, *Aleksei Gan*, p. 11. These collections were fully nationalised and amalgamated in November 1918.

39. *Aleksandr Rodchenko: Experiments for the Future*, p. 80.

40. *Anarkhiya* was published in Moscow from September 1917 until July 1918, by Aba and Zeev Gordin. It was edited by V. V. Barmash. For details, see A. D. Sarab'yanov, "Stat'i v gazete 'Anarkhiya' (1918)", in Kazimir Malevich, *Sobranie sochinenii v pyati tomakh*, ed. A. S. Shatskikh (Moscow: Gileya, 1995), vol. 1, pp. 330-332; and Nina

Gourianova, *The Aesthetics of Anarchy: Art and Ideology in the Early Russian Avant-Garde* (Berkeley, Los Angeles and London: University of California Press, 2012), pp. 220ff.

41. See A. Gan, "Revolyutsiya i narodnyi teatr", *Anarkhiya*, no. 12 (March 1918); and Sarab'yanov, "Stat'i v gazete 'Anarkhiya' (1918)", p. 331.

42. See Sarab'yanov, "Stat'i v gazete 'Anarkhiya' (1918)", pp. 330-332.

43. A. Gan, A. Morgunov and K. Malevich, "Zadachi iskusstva i rol' dushitelei iskusstva", *Anarkhiya*, no. 26 (23 March 1918); English translation in Kazimir S. Malevich, *Essays On Art 1915-1933*, ed. Troels Andersen, trans. Xenia Glowacki-Prus and Arnold McMillin (Copenhagen: Borgen, 1968), vol. 1, pp. 49-50.

44. See, for instance, A. Gan, "Osobnyak Morozova", *Anarkhiya*, no. 21 (19 March 1918); and Sarab'yanov, "Stat'i v gazete 'Anarkhiya' (1918)", pp. 332, 337.

45. Advertisement, *Anarkhiya*, no. 72 (30 May 1918); cited in Gourianova, *The Aesthetics of Anarchy*, p. 225.

46. A *Slap in the Face of Public Taste* was the Futurists' manifesto of 1912. See D. Burliuk, Aleksandr [Aleksei] Kruchenykh, V. Mayakovskii, Viktor [sic.] Khlebnikov, "Poshchechina obshchestvennomu vkusu", in *Poshchechina obshchestvennomu vkusu* (Moscow: G. L. Kuzmin, 1912); English translation in Anna Lawton, ed., *Russian Futurism through its Manifestoes, 1912-1928* (Ithaca and London: Cornell University Press, 1988), pp. 51-2.

47. Aleksei Gan, "Na obshchestvennom mitinge 7 yunya", *Anarkhiya*, no. 85 (15 June 1918); English translation adapted from Gourianova, *The Aesthetics of Anarchy*, p. 224.

48. Stepanova, *Chelovek*, p. 66. The maximalists were an extreme wing of the Party of Socialist Revolutionaries.

49. Romberg, "Tektonika".

50. *Prikazy Moskovskogo Okruzhenogo Komissariata po voennym delam* (Moscow), 2 May 1919 – 27 December 1920, cited in Cooke, "Sources of a Radical Mission", pp. 29-30.

51. See *Prikazy*; Cooke, "Sources of a Radical Mission", pp. 29-30.

52. B. K[ushner], "Kommunisty-Futuristy", *Iskusstvo kommuny* (Petrograd), no. 9 (2 February 1919), p. 3; and "Organizatsiya Komfutov", *Iskusstvo kommuny*, no. 8 (26 January 1919), p. 3.

53. A. Valyuzhenich, *O. M. Brik. Materialy i biografii* (Moscow: Niva, 1993), p. 221.

54. See I. Vakar and T. Mikhienko, eds., *Malevich o sebe. Pis'ma. Dokumenty. Vospominaniya. Kritika* (Moscow: RA, 2004), vol. 1, p. 140.

55. Stepanova, *Chelovek*, p. 104.

56. See Gan and Malevich's request for tickets to attend the Museum Conference, 11-18 February 1919, Petrograd, in *Malevich o sebe*, vol. 1, p. 416.

57. Stepanova, *Chelovek*, p. 104.

58. Stepanova, *Chelovek*, p. 67.

59. Varst, "Rabochii klub. Konstruktivist A. M. Rodchenko", *SA*, no. 1 (1926), p. 36; Kazimir Malevich, "Pis'mo k redaktsiyu", *SA*, no. 5 (1928), p. 156; and K. Malevich "Forma, tsvet i oshchushchenie", ibid., pp. 157-159.

60. See *Malevich o sebe*, vol. 1, p. 108.

61. Stepanova, *Chelovek*, p. 65.

62. See A. A. Sidorov, "Khudozhestvennye vystavki", *Tvorchestvo*, no. 2-4 (1920), p. 34; reprinted in *Malevich o sebe*, vol. 2, p. 526.

63. See Mikhail Meilkh, "Chelovek ochen' srodnyi poezii...", pp. 45-6; cited in *Malevich o sebe*, vol. 1, p. 125.

64. Malevich, letter to Aleksei Kruchenykh, [18 September 1920], in *Malevich o sebe*, vol. 1, p. 129; and Stepanova, *Chelovek*, p. 109. In his letter to Kruchenykh, Malevich referred to Unovis as "Affirmation of the New Art" (*utverzhdenie novogo iskusstva*), a term which emphasises the function of his new group. The group itself, however, was registered as "Affirmers" or "Champions of the new Art" (*Utverditeli novogo iskusstva*). See *Malevich o sebe*, vol. 1, p. 442-444. I am indebted to Maria Kokkori for pointing this out.

65. Kazimir Malevich, "Suprematizm kak Unovisskoe dokazatel'stvo", manuscript, [late 1921- early 1922], private archive, St Petersburg; printed in Malevich, *Sobranie sochinenii*, vol. 5, pp. 195-199; English translation, "Suprematism as Unovis Proof", in *Russian Avant-Garde 1910-1930: The George Costakis Collection: Theory – Criticism* (Athens: Ministry of Culture, National Gallery and Alexandros Soutzos Museum; and Delphi: European Cultural Centre of Delphi, 1996) p. 571. Malevich wrote this text for a collection of articles "From Representation to Construction" ("Ot izobrazheniya k konstruktsii"), planned by Moscow's Institute of Artistic Culture (*Institut khudozhestvennoi kul'tury* – Inkhuk).

66. A. I. Konopleva, "Aleksei Mikhailovich Gan", *Kinovedcheskie zapiski*, no. 49 (2006), pp. 212-221.

67. A. M. Gan, A. M. Rodchenko and V. F. Stepanova, "Kto my. Manifest gruppy kon-

struktivistov", [1922], typescript, Rodchenko-Stepanova Archive, Moscow; reprinted in Aleksandr Rodchenko, *Opyty dlya budushchego. Dnevniki. Stat'i. Pis'ma. Zapiski* (Moscow: Grant', 1996), pp. 127-129; English translation in *Aleksandr Rodchenko: Experiments for the Future*, pp. 143-145.

68. See Aleksei Gan, "Spravka o Kazimire Maleviche", *SA*, no. 3 (1927), pp. 104, 106; reprinted in *Malevich o sebe*, vol. 2, pp. 539-541; English translation as "Notes on Kazimir Malevich", in *Architectural Design* (London) vol. 5, no.5/6 (1989), pp. 35-36.

69. AlexejGan,"KasimirMalewitsch",*MoskauerRundschau*(Moscow),(24November1929).

The Working Group of Constructivists

70. Stepanova, *Chelovek*, pp. 93, 108.

71. Stepanova, *Chelovek*, p. 108.

72. Stepanova, *Chelovek*, p. 92.

73. Stepanova, *Chelovek*, p. 93.

74. A. Gan "Front khudozhestvennogo truda. Materialy k Vserossiiskoi konferentsii levykh v iskusstve. Konstruktivisty", *Ermitazh* (Moscow), no. 13 (1922), p. 3.

75. Gan "Front khudozhestvennogo truda", p. 3.

76. "Report No. 1", 1921, Rodchenko-Stepanova archive; English translation in S. O. Khan-Magomedov, *Rodchenko: The Complete Work* (London: Thames and Hudson, 1986), p. 290.

77. See Aleksei Gan, "'O programme i plane rabot Gruppy konstruktivistov", in S. O. Khan-Magomedov, *INKhUK i rannyi konstruktivizm* (Moscow: Architectura, 1994), pp. 98-9; and "Report No. 2", Khan-Magomedov, *Rodchenko*, p. 290.

78. Khan-Magomedov, *Rodchenko*, n. 14, pp. 92-3.

79. For various statements made by the Constructivists in the course of their discussions, see Khan-Magomedov, *Rodchenko*, p. 92; Khan-Magomedov, *INKhUK i rannii konstruktivizm*, p. 103; *Art into Life: Russian Constructivism 1914-1932* (Henry Art Gallery, Seattle, WA.; and New York: Rizzoli, 1990), pp. 67ff; and Maria Gough, *The Artist as Producer: Russian Constructivism in Revolution* (Berkeley, Los Angeles, London: University of California Press, 2005), pp. 71-73.

80. "Programme of the Working Group of Constructivists of Inkhuk" in Khan-Magomedov, *Rodchenko*, p. 290. The programme was published in 1922 (Gan, "Front khudozhestvennogo truda"), and elaborated in Gan's book (*Konstruktivizm*: Tver' 1922) reviewed by V. Zhemchuzhnyi, "Aleksei Gan 'Konstruktivizm'", *Ermitazh*, no. 9 (1922), p. 8.

81. "Programme of the Working Group of Constructivists of Inkhuk" in Khan-Magomedov, *Rodchenko*,p. 290.

Constructivism 1922

82. In 1922, Rodchenko and Gan had apparently worked on a book about Constructivism and the plan has survived (Rodchenko-Stepanova archive, Moscow, cited in Lavrent'ev, *Aleksei Gan*, p. 70):
1. Painting – paths and stages. *Faktura* and its mechanisms. Pictorial space – as an entry into real space. Linear space.
2. Instruments and means of production 1) Preamble; 2) Line – element; 3) Space.
3. Constructivism. Aims and achievements in production.
4. Execution of orders. Curtains, emblems. Tea service. Lamps. Kiosk. Production of *My*. Design for the house of Soviets (plan, façade and cross-section).

83. Aleksandr Grishchenko and Aleksandr Shevchenko, "'Tsvetodinamos' i 'Tektonicheskii primitivism'", *Dvenadtsataya Gosudarstvennaya vystavka. Tsvetodinamos i tektonicheskii primitivizm* (Moscow: Otdel IZO NKP, VTsVB, 1919); reprinted in I. Matsa, ed., *Sovetskoe iskusstvo za 15 let. Materialy i dokumentatsiya* (Moscow and Leningrad: Gosizdat, 1933), pp. 117-120.

84. See Romberg, "Tektonika".

85. S. I. Ozhegov, *Slovar' russkogo yazyka* (Moscow: *Sovetskaya entsiklopediya*, 1972), p. 727.

86. Aleksei Gan, *Konstruktivizm* (Tver': Tverskoe izdatel'stvo, 1922), p. 61.

87. Gan, *Konstruktivizm*, p. 61.

88. See Vladimir Dal', *Tolkovyi slovar' zhivogo velikorusskogo yazyka* (St Petersburg and Moscow: Izdanie knigoprodavtsa-tipografa M. O. Vol'fa, 1882), vol. 4, p. 404.

89. Romberg "Tektonika".

90. "Programme of the Working Group of Constructivists", in Khan-Magomedov, *Rodchenko*, p. 290.

91. Gan, *Konstruktivizm*, p. 61.

92. Stepanova, *Chelovek*, p. 168

93. See David Burliuk, "Kubizm" and "Faktura" in *Poshchechina obshchestvennomu vkusu* (Moscow, 1912), pp. 95-101, and 102-110. For a translation of "Cubism", see Bowlt *Russian Art of the Avant-Garde*, pp. 70-77.

94. Burliuk, "Faktura".

95. Vladimir Markov, *Printsipy tvorchestva v plasticheskikh iskusstvakh. Faktura* (St Petersburg: Union of Youth, 1914).

96. I am indebted to Maria Kokkori for this information.

97. Tatlin showed his "synthetic and static compositions" (*sintezo-statichnykh kompozitsii*) in his studio at 37 Ostozhenka Street, Moscow, on 10-14 May 1914. He later called this "The First Exhibition of Painterly Reliefs". See Anatoli Strigalev and Jürgen Harten, eds., *Vladimir Tatlin: Retrospektive* (Cologne: DuMont Buchverlag, 1993), p. 386. Strigalev divides the reliefs into three groups – painterly, spatial and corner reliefs (ibid., p. 33, note 37). Both Markov and Tatlin employed similar terms *nabor materialov* and *materialnyi podbor* respectively, although both are rendered as "Selection of Materials" in English.

98. See, for instance, Nikolai Punin, *Pamyatnik III internatsionala* (Petrograd: IZO, NKP, 1921); and Lodder, *Russian Constructivism*, p 65.

99. "Programme of the Working Group of Constructivists", Khan-Magomedov, *Rodchenko*, p. 290.

100. See Dal', *Tolkovyi slovar'*, vol. 2, p. 152; and D. N. Ushakov ed., *Tolkovyi slovar' russkogo yazyka* (Moscow: Sovetskaya entsikopediya, 1935), vol. 1, p. 1443.

101. See Albert Gleizes and Jean Metzinger, *Du "Cubisme"* (Paris: Eugene Figuière, 1912); English translation in Edward Fry, *Cubism* (London: Thames and Hudson, 1978), p. 107.

102. Vladimir Markov, "Printsipy novogo iskusstva", *Soyuz molodezhi* (St Petersburg), no. 1 (April 1912), pp. 5-14, no. 2 (June 1912), pp. 5-18; English translation in Bowlt, *Russian Art of the Avant-Garde*, pp. 25-38.

103. Ivan Puni, "Tvorchestvo zhizni", *Iskusstvo kommuny*, no. 5 (5 January 1919), p. 1.

104. See V. Dmitriev, "Pervyi itog", *Iskusstvo kommuny*, no. 15 (16 March 1919), p. 3.

105. Ushakov, *Tolkovyi slovar'*, vol. 3, 1939, p. 648.

106. Lyubov' Popova, statement in *Desyataya Gosudarstvennaya vystavka* (Moscow, 1918); reprinted in Matsa, *Sovetskoe iskusstvo*, p. 112. In the same statement, she also used the term *akonstruktivnost'* to denote the absence of construction and hence the antithesis of architectonics (*arkhitektonika*). Artists also used the terms *zhivopisnoe postroenie* or *zhivopisnyi stroi* and even *struktura* to denote pictorial structure.

107. See *Desyataya Gosudarstvennaya vystavka*, in Matsa, *Sovetskoe iskusstvo*, p. 113.

108. *XIX vystavka VTsVB* (Moscow: Otdel IZO Narkomprosa, 1920), nos. 93-107 and 117.

109. See "Protokol zasedaniya Inkhuka", 1 January 1921 and 21 January 1921, Rodchenko-Stepanova archive, Moscow.

110. Gan, "Bor'ba za 'Massovoe Deistvo'", p. 49.

111. "Programme of the Working Group of Constructivists", in Khan-Magomedov, *Rodchenko*, p. 290.

112. Aleksei Gan, "Konstruktivizm v poligrafii", *SA*, no. 3 (1928), p. 80.

113. Gan, "Konstruktivizm v poligrafii", p. 80.

Extending Constructivism: *Kino-Fot*

114. The first issue of *Kino-Fot* seems to have gone to the printers on 23 August 1922. See Aleksei Gan, letter to Esfir Shub, 23 August 1922, RGALI, fond 3035, op. 1, ed. khr. 105; reprinted in Zabrodina, "'... Bolezn' moya innogo poryadka'".
Gan planned a book of essays also to be called *Kino-Fot*, which would reproduce material already published in the journal as well as additional texts, including articles by Stepanova and Rodchenko. See Gan, untitled prospectus, [1923], Stepanova-Rodchenko archive, Moscow, cited in Lavrent'ev, *Aleksei Gan*, p. 116. Gan had also prepared no. 7 of the journal, although this never appeared and has not come to light.

115. Aleksei Gan, *Da zdravstvuet demonstratsiya byta!* (Moscow, 1923).

116. The following works by Rodchenko were reproduced in *Kino-Fot*: issue no. 1 – a painting (1917), drawing (1915), and three collages; no. 2 – two spatial constructions (1919 & 1920); no. 3 – drawing of a building for the Soviet Deputies, and two photomontages; no. 4 – a kiosk design (1920), a spatial construction (1921); no. 5 – a design for a kiosk, two spatial constructions (1918 & 1920), and five graphic designs for *Kino-Pravda* intertitles.

117. See *Kino-Fot*, no. 3 (19-25 September 1922), cover and pp. 2-6.

118. Aleksei Gan, "Kinematograf i kinematografiya", *Kino-Fot*, no. 1 (25-31 August 1922), p. 1; English translation in Richard Taylor and Ian Christie, eds., *The Film Factory: Russian and Soviet Cinema in Documents* (Cambridge, MA.: Harvard University Press, 1988), pp. 67-68.

119. "Programme of the Working Group of Constructivists of Inkhuk", in Khan-Magomedov, *Rodchenko*, p. 290.

120. Gan, *Konstruktivizm*, p. 36.

121. A. V. Lunacharskii, "Zadachi gosudarstvennogo kinodela v RSFSR" in *Kinematograf. Sbornik statei* (Moscow, 1919), pp. 5-7; English translation in Taylor and Christie, *The Film Factory*, pp. 47-49.

122. Vladimir Lenin, "Directive on Cinema Affairs"; English translation in Taylor and Christie, *The Film Factory*, p. 56.

123. See Christina Lodder, "Promoting Constructivism: *Kino-Fot* and Rodchenko's Move into Photography", *History of Photography* (London), vol.24, no.4 (Winter 2000), pp. 292-299; reprinted in Lodder, *Constructive Strands in Russian Art*, pp. 368-391.

124. Rodchenko's photomontages *Psikhologiya* and *Detektiv* (*Psychology* and *The Detective*, both of 1922) were reproduced in *Kino-Fot*, no. 3 (19-25 September 1922), pp. 11-12.

125. See E. Shub, *Krupnym planom* (Moscow, 1959).

126. N. Kalinina, ed., "Ol'-Ga-lina iz Chichago", *Da*, no. 2-3 (1995), p. 47; cited in Lavrent'ev, *Aleksei Gan*.

127. See Esfir Shub, "O sebe", in *Zhizn' moya – kinematograf* (Moscow: Iskusstvo, 1972), p. 244.

128. Dziga Vertov, "My. Variant manifesta", *Kino-Fot*, no. 1 (25-31 August 1922), pp. 11-12; and L. B. Kuleshov, "Iskusstvo, sovremennaya zhizn' i KINEMATOGRAFIYA", *Kino-Fot*, no. 1 (25-31 August 1922), p. 2.

129. See Gan "Kinematograf i kinematografiya", p. 1; Taylor and Christie, *The Film Factory*, pp., 67-68.

130. A. G.[Aleksei Gan], "Kino-Pravda. Trinadtsatyi opyt", *Kino-Fot*, no. 5 (10 December 1922), pp. 6-7; English translation in Taylor and Christie, *The Film Factory*, p. 78.

131. Rodchenko's inter-titles illustrate "*Kino-Pravda*. Trinadtsatyi opyt", pp. 6-7.

132. Lyudvig Gil'berseimer [Ludwig Hilberseimer], "Dinamicheskaya zhivopis'", *Kino-Fot*, no. 1 (25-31 August 1922), p. 7.

133. Lyudvig Gil'berseimer [Ludwig Hilberseimer], "Dinamicheskaya zhivopis'. (Bespredmetnyi kinematograf.)", *Veshch'/Gegenstand/Objet* (Berlin), no. 3 (May 1922), pp. 17-19.

134. See *Veshch'/Gegenstand/Objet* (Berlin), no. 1-2 (March-April 1922), p. 28. Egling's first name had been corrected from Richard to Viking by issue no. 3.
See ibid., p. 18.

135. Gan, *Konstruktivizm*, p. 69-70.

Constructivism and Architecture: *Sovremennaya arkhitektura* – SA

136. Cooke, "Sources of a radical mission", p. 13. Cooke provides a detailed examination of Gan's ideas about architecture within the context of current architectural discourse and practice.

137. Gan, *Konstruktivizm*, p. 63.

138. Gan, *Konstruktivizm*, p. 64.

139. Gan, *Konstruktivizm*, p. 60.

140. Aleksei Gan. "Kommunisticheskii gorod. (V planovykh razrobotkakh konstruktivistov)", *Teatral'naya Moskva* (Moscow), no. 40 (1922), pp. 5-6.

141. See M. Ya. Ginzburg, *Stil' i epokha. Problemy sovremennoi arkhitektury* (Moscow: Gosudarstvennoe izdatel'stvo, 1924), figs. XLI and XLII.

142. The editorial board was quite large and included, among others, Andrei Burov, Aleksandr Vesnin, Viktor Vesnin, Ginzburg, and Ilya Golosov.

143. See for instance, Aleksei Gan, "Chto takoe konstruktivizm ?", *SA*, no. 3 (1928), pp. 79-81; which dealt with Constructivist graphics and cinema.

144. Aleksei Gan, "Novomu teatru – novoe zdanie", *SA*, no. 3 (1927), p. 81.

145. See, for instance, Varst, "Rabochii klub. Konstruktivist A. M. Rodchenko", *SA*, no. 1 (1926), p. 36; "Konstruktivizm v reklame", *SA*, no. 2 (1926), inside back cover; "Konstruktivizm v armature dnevnogo byta" *SA*, no. 2 inside cover; Aleksei Gan, "Fakty za nas", *SA*, no. 2, (1926), p. 39; Gan, "Spravka o Maleviche"; and Andrei Novikov, "Derevenskii kiosk. Proekt – maket. Konstruktivist A. M. Gan", *SA*, no. 1 (1926), p. 35.

146. K. Malevich, "Forma, tsvet i oshchushchenie", *SA*, no. 5 (1928), pp. 157-159; English translation in *Architectural Design*, vol. 5, no. 5/6 (1989), pp. 45-47; and I. Klyun, "Kubizm kak zhivipisnyi method", *SA*, no. 6 (1928), pp. 194-199.

147. Editorial statement, *SA*, no. 5 (1928), p. 156; English translation in *Architectural Design*, vol. 5, no. 5/6 (1989), p. 33.

148. Editorial statement, *SA*, no. 5 (1928).

149. Editorial statement, *SA*, no. 5 (1928).

150. Gan, "Spravka o Kazimire Maleviche", p. 106.

The theory and Practice of Constructivist Typography

151. Aleksei Gan, description of his work on *Anarchy* in 1918 in the caption to its display as exhibit 157 at *The First Discussional Exhibition of Associations of Active Revolutionary Art*. See *1-aya diskussionnaya vystavka ob'edinenii aktivnogo revolyutsionnogo iskusstva* (Moscow, 1924).

152. Aleksei Gan, description of his book *Constructivism* in the caption to its display as exhibit 158 at *The First Discussional Exhibition*. See *1-aya diskussionnaya vystavka.*

153. Aleksei Gan, description of *Kino-Fot* in the caption to its display as exhibit 159 at the *The First Discussional Exhibition*. See *1-aya diskussionnaya vystavka.*

154. Aleksei Gan, "Konstruktivizm v nabore i verstke", *SA*, no. 2 (1926), inside back cover.

155. Lavrent'ev, *Aleksei Gan,* p. 90.

156. Aleksei Gan, "Stennaya gazeta", ms, undated [1920s], Rodchenko-Stepanova Archive, Moscow, cited in Lavrent'ev, *Aleksei Gan*, p. 90.

157. Aleksei Gan, "Zadacha stengaza", 1921, manuscript, Rodchenko-Stepanova archive, Moscow, cited in Lavrent'ev, *Aleksei Gan*, pp. 135-136.

158. He wrote, "the first mobilisation of typographical material in the newspaper of 1918". See *1-aya diskussionaya vystavka.*

159. See, for instance, Lodder, *Russian Constructivism*, plate VII; and figs. 5.30, 5.31, 5.33, pp. 170-173.

160. *Kino-Fot*, no. 1 (25-31 August 1920), p. 1.

161. Charlie Chaplin was not only popular because he represented the ordinary person against the world, but also because of the innovative quality of his movements on film, which were like the Taylorised gestures favoured by Russian innovators like Meyerkhold. See Yu. Tsiv'yan, "O Chapline v russkom avangarde i o zakonakh sluchainogo v iskusstve", *NLO* [*Novoe Literaturnoe Obozrenie*] (Moscow) no. 81 (2006), pp. 99-129.

162. Lavrent'ev, *Aleksei Gan*, p. 115.

163. See Christina Lodder, "Aleksandr Rodchenko, Aleksei Gan and the Emergence of Constructivist Typography", in Lodder, *Constructive Strands in Russian Art* (London: Pindar Press, 2005), pp. 392-425.

164. Gan, *Konstruktivizm*, p. 18.

165. Aleksei Gan, "Konstruktivizm v tipografskom proizvodstve", *Almanakh proletkul'ta* (Moscow, 1925), p. 119.

166. I am indebted to Ellen Lupton for this information.

167. El Lissitzky, "Kniga s tochke zreniya zretiel'nogo vospriyatiya – visual'naya kniga", *Iskusstvo knigi* (Moscow) no. 3 (1962), p. 167.
Gan's authorship of *Constructivism*'s design has been challenged. Khan-Magomedov has asserted that Rodchenko designed the cover on the basis of a drawing for it, which is still in the family's collection. See Khan-Magomedov, *Rodchenko*, p. 131. This overlays one set of letters in one typeface, i.e. the title over the letters of the author's name, which are printed in another colour and typeface. In this respect, the design is very different from the one that was actually used, both in terms of the typefaces employed and the organisation. Moreover, the style of the cover is very different from any other produced by Rodchenko around this time. He tended to use the entirety of the surface of the cover. This is certainly not true of Gan's *Constructiv-*

ism, which suggests that Gan alone was responsible for the design of the covers and layout of this pioneering Constructivist text. In this respect it is worth noting that Khan-Magomedov does not mention the internal layout of the book.

168. Lavrent'ev, *Aleksei Gan*, p. 110.

169. Lavrent'ev, *Aleksei Gan*, p. 119.

170. Aleksei Gan, "Konstruktivizm v tipografskom proizvodstve", in *Almanakh proletkul'ta* (Moscow, 1925), p. 117.

171. Gan, "Konstruktivizm v tipografskom proizvodstve", p. 119.

Gan as an Industrial Designer

172. Gan, *Konstruktivizm*, p. 64. The statement is in bold in the original.

173. Aleksei Gan, "Fakty za nas", *SA*, no. 2 (1926), p. 39.

174. Gan, "Fakty za nas", p. 39,

175. This is the caption Moisei Ginzburg gave the kiosk stand and it is also spelt out in the large lettering at the top. See Ginzburg, *Stil' i epokha*, plate XVI and XVII.

176. Lavrent'ev, *Aleksei Gan*, p. 153.

177. Lavrent'ev, *Aleksei Gan*, p. 155.

178. See Gan, *Konstruktivizm*, p. 69. *L'Esprit Nouveau* was edited by Le Corbusier, while *Veshch'* also contained articles about architecture, see, for instance, Korbyus'e Son'e, "Sovremennaya arkhitektura", *Veshch'/Gegendstand/Objet* (Berlin), no. 1-2 (March-April 1922), pp. 20-22. Gan reprinted Lyudvig Gil'berseimer, "Dinamicheskaya zhivopis'. (Bespredmetnyi kinematograf.)", *Veshch'/Gegenstand/Objet*, no. 3 (May 1922), pp. 17-19 in *Kino-Fot*, no. 1 (25-31 August 1922), p. 7.

179. Andrei Novikov, "Derevenskii kiosk. Proekt-maket. Konstruktivist Aleksei Gan", *SA*, no. 1 (1926), p. 35.

180. Novikov, "Derevenskii kiosk", p. 35.

181. Gan, "Fakty za nas", p. 39.

Gan and Constructivist Cinema

182. See Romberg, "Labor Demonstrations" for a full and interesting examination of *The Island of the Young Pioneers*.

183. Aleksei Gan, "Kino ne teatr", *Teatral'naya Moskva*, no. 45 (1922), p. 12.

184. Gan, *Da zdravstvuet demonstratsiya byta!*, p. 10.

185. Gan, *Da zdravstvuet demonstratsiya byta!*, p. 4.

186. Gan, *Da zdravstvuet demonstratsiya byta!*, p. 11.

187. See Romberg, "Labor Demonstrations". Vertov apparently gave Gan the money to make his film out of his own budget.

188. Lavrent'ev, *Aleksei Gan*, p. 117; and Romberg, "Labor Demonstrations".

189. Lavrent'ev, *Aleksei Gan*, p. 117.

190. Aleksei Gan, "Da zdravstvuet demonstratsiya byta!", *Proletkino*, no. 4-5 (August 1924), p. 18; cited in Romberg, "Labor Demonstrations".

191. See Romberg, "Labor Demonstrations".

192. Romberg, "Labor Demonstrations"; and Lavrent'ev, *Aleksei Gan*, p. 126.

193. Aleksei Gan, "Za organizatsiyu faktov zhizni", *Sovetskii ekran*, no. 15 (13 April 1926), p. 5.

Keeping the Constructivist Flame Alive

194. Gan, *Konstruktivizm*, p. 69.

195. Gan, *Konstruktivizm*, pp. 69-70.

196. Boris Arvatov, "Veshch'", *Pechat', i revolyutsiya* (Moscow), no. 4 (1922), p. 342.

197. See *Katalog vystavki. Konstruktivisty K. K. Medunetskii, V. A. Stenberg, G. A. Stenberg* (Moscow: Kafe Poetov, 1922).

198. Gan presents the group as The First Working Group of Constructivists in *Constructivism*.

199. Nikolai Kupreyanov, letter to Nikolai Punin, 5 February 1923, reprinted in N. Punin, *Mir svetel lubov'yu. Dnevniki. Pis'ma*, ed. L. A. Zykova (Moscow: Artist. Rezhisser. Teatr, 2000), p. 171.

200. Lavrent'ev, *Aleksei Gan*, p. 128.

201. *1-ya diskussionnaya vystavka* .

202. Aleksandr Rodchenko, letter to Varvara Stepanova, 21 May 1925; English translation in *Aleksandr Rodchenko: Experiments for the Future*, p. 177.

203. Aleksandr Rodchenko, letter to Varvara Stepanova, 6 June 1925; English translation in

Aleksandr Rodchenko: Experiments for the Future, p. 183.

204. Lavrent'ev, *Aleksei Gan*, p. 118.

205. Varvara Stepanova, letter to Aleksandr Rodchenko, 16 May 1925; English translation in *Aleksandr Rodchenko: Experiments for the Future*, p. 176.

206. Aleksei Gan, letter to Esfir Shub, 16 August 1925; reprinted in Zabrodina, "'… Bolezn' moya innogo poryadka", p. 223.

207. See "Deklaratsiya", in *SA*. no. 3 (March 1928), pp. 73-74; and "Dekaratsiya ob'edineniya 'Oktyabr'", in P. I. Novitskii ed., *Izofront. Klasssovaya bor'ba na fronte prostranstvennykh iskusstv* (Moscow and Leningrad, 1931), pp. 135-142; English translation in Bowlt, *Russian Art of the Avant-Garde*, pp. 274-279.

208. Aleksandr Lavrent'ev, "V. F. Stepanova o rannem konstruktivizme", *Teknicheskaya estetika* (*Trudy VNIITE*), no. 21 (1979), pp. 116-117.

LIST OF ILLUSTRATIONS

p. XXXIV Aleksei Gan, *Long Live the Demonstration of Life!* (Moscow, 1923). Cover designed by Aleksei Gan.

pp. XXXVI-XXXIX Inside spreads of *Kino-fot*, no. 3 (19-25 September 1922), designed by Aleksei Gan, showing a sketch for a building for the Council of Deputies (Sovdepa), 1920, by Aleksandr Rodchenko and drawings of Charlie Chaplin by Varvara Stepanova.

pp. XLII-XLIII Inside layout of *Kino-fot*, no. 5 (10 December 1922), illustrating Aleksandr Rodchenko's intertitles for Dziga Vertov's newsreel, *Kino-Pravda*.

p. XLIV *SA: Sovremennaya arkhitektura*, no. 3 (1928), front cover designed by Aleksei Gan.

pp. XLVI-XLVII *SA: Sovremennaya arkhitektura*, no. 1 (1928), back and front cover designed by Aleksei Gan.

p. L Gan working on the cover of the journal *Technology and Life* (*Tekhnika i zhizn'*) in the studio of Aleksandr Rodchenko and Varvara Stepanova, 1924. Photograph by Aleksandr Rodchenko. A. Rodchenko & V. Stepanova Archive, Moscow.

pp. LIV-LV *SA: Sovremennaya arkhitektura*, no. 3 (1927), pp. 96-97, designed by Aleksei Gan, concerning *The First Exhibition of Contemporary Architecture*.

p. LVIII-LIX *SA: Sovremennaya arkhitektura*, no. 1 (1928), pp. 4-5, inside spread designed by Aleksei Gan, illustrating Viktor and Aleksandr Vesnins' project for the House of Production and Commerce in Sverdlovsk (1927) and Ivan Leonidov's project for a film studio 1927.

p. LX Above: Aleksei Gan, Design for a Folding Sales Stand, produced for the Moscow Association of Businesses for Processing Products of the Agricultural Industry (Mossel'prom), 1922. Reproduced in Aleksei Gan, 'Fakty za nas', *SA: Sovremennaya arkhitektura*, no. 2 (1926), p. 39.
Below: Sales stand on a Moscow street, 1928, displaying features in common with Gan's design. Photograph by Aleksandr Rodchenko. A. Rodchenko & V. Stepanova Archive, Moscow.

p. LXII Above: Aleksei Gan, Kiosk for the sale of books, magazines and stationary materials, c. 1922-1923, designed for All Russian Committee for Help to War Invalids (Vserokompom). Shown in its closed state. Reproduced in M. Ya. Ginzburg, *Style and the Epoch: Problems of Contemporary Architecture* (*Stil' i epokha. Problemy sovremennoi arkhitektury*; Moscow, 1924), Fig. LVI.
Below: Aleksei Gan, Kiosk for the sale of books, magazines and stationary materials, c. 1922-1923, designed for All Russian Committee for help to War Invalids (Vserokompom). Shown in its open state. Reproduced in M. Ya. Ginzburg, *Style and the Epoch* (*Stil' i epokha*; Moscow, 1924), Fig. LVII.

p. LXIV Aleksei Gan, Design for a Rural Kiosk, 1925, commissioned by *The Peasant Newspaper* (*Krestyanskaya gazeta*). Reproduced in Andrei Novikov, 'Derevenskii kiosk. Proekt-maket. Konstruktivist Aleksei Gan,' SA*: Sovremennnaya arkhitektura*, no. 1 (1926), p. 35.

p. LXVI Aleksei Gan looking at film footage, 1924. Photograph by Aleksandr Rodchenko, A. Rodchenko & V. Stepanova Archive, Moscow.

p. LXVIII Aleksei Gan holding a mirror in which his wife Esfir Shub is reflected. Photograph by Aleksandr Rodchenko, A. Rodchenko & V. Stepanova Archive, Moscow.

Back flap *SA: Sovremennaya arkhitektura,* no. 2 (1927), front and back cover designed by Aleksei Gan.

SA: Sovremennaya arkhitektura, no. 3 (1927), front and back cover designed by Aleksei Gan.

SA: Sovremennaya arkhitektura, no. 4-5 (1927). Front cover designed by Aleksei Gan, marking the tenth anniversary of the October Revolution of 1917, and indicating the exceptional nature of the issue by including a partial image of Ivan Leonidov's project for the Lenin Institute and Library(1927). Back cover designed by Aleksei Gan, advertising the *First Exhibition of Contemporary Architecture*, which opened on 18 June 1927.

АЛЕКСЕЙ ГАН

КОНСТРУКТИВИЗМ

ALEKSEI GAN.

CONSTRUCTIVISM.

Printed by the Second State Printing House
R. Ts. 357. Tiz. No. 249.
Edition 2000, Tver 1922

Constructivism is a phenomenon of our days. It emerged in 1920 among left-wing painters and the theorists of "mass action".

The present publication is an agitational book, with which the constructivists are beginning the fight against the supporters of traditional art.

Moscow 1922

We declare uncompromising war on art!

The 1st Working Group of Constructivists
1920
Moscow.

Long live

The Communist Expression

of Material

Structures!

The 1st Working Group of Constructivists
1921
Moscow.

“Undoubtedly,” it will be said, “religious, moral, philosophical, and juridicial ideas have been modified in the course of historical development. But religion, morality, philosophy, political science, and law, constantly survived this change.”

“There are, besides, eternal truths, such as Freedom, Justice, etc., that are common to all states of society. But communism abolishes eternal truths, it abolishes all religion, and all morality, instead of constituting them on a new basis; it therefore acts in contradiction to all past historical experience.”

What does this accusation reduce itself to?

The history of all past society has consisted in the development of class antagonisms, antagonisms that assumed different forms at different epochs.

But whatever form they may have taken, one fact is common to all past ages, viz., the exploitation of one part of society by the other. No wonder, then, that the social consciousness of past ages, despite all the multiplicity and variety it displays, moves within certain common forms, or general ideas, which cannot completely vanish except with the total disappearance of class antagonism.

(The Communist Manifesto).

Revolutionary Marxist thought
in words, but chronic incapacity in action.

Revolutionary Marxist thinking revealed the dynamic force of history, developed the theory of historical materialism, and established that "each stage of social development must be understood in terms of its particular characteristics and only in terms of its particular characteristics", but it has been silenced by the quagmire of aesthetic dogmatism.

The relationship between the substructure and superstructure, i.e. the change in the superstructure as a result of changes in the relations of production —all this is forgotten as soon as a communist confronts beauty. **He becomes strange and submissive.**

The sacred and incorruptible gifts of aesthetics make him weak.

He becomes a typical intellectual —and "the concept of dynamism" and "the philosophy of action" cease to be his idea or his philosophy.

Why is this?

The fact is that while we are ruthlessly and brutally attacking the bulwarks of capitalism and its way of life, and are trying to restructure the entire social order in the direction of communism, in the field of so-called art we are turning back to epochs that were less perfect, more crude, and in essence extremely anti-communist.

It is true that as the process of struggle grows more severe, the atmosphere in the premises of our departments directing artistic affairs becomes cleaner.

The kings and wizards of the beautiful become quieter, and their patrons become quieter with them.

But we only had to liquidate the military front of the Civil War, and then move on to peaceful construction, for the manufacturers of art once again to raise their heads, and our cultural activists to open their agitational mouths and spread inflammatory words about the eternal values of the beautiful.

It turns out that new victories on the revolutionary front bring new defeats on the front of intellectual endeavour.

Having consolidated our achievement in the field of politics and having moved on to the revolutionary tasks of reorganising the national economy, our revolution is now making an abrupt turn and under the banner of academicism is trying to enslave intellectual production and its producers.

From outside, it almost goes unnoticed.

We lack Marxist literacy.

The absence of an elementary Marxist education is evident even among politically reliable party comrades.

Moreover, our so-called qualified communists sometimes treat questions about which they know little in an extremely thoughtless and reckless way.

All of this has a lethal effect on our activity, our thinking, our approach to the varied and multi-faceted phenomena of life, and on the solutions to a whole series of questions that arise in connection with the building of communism and the communist way of life.

As soon as we approach art, we stop being Marxists.

In *The Poverty of Philosophy*, Marx states, "The theoreticians of the proletariat must set themselves the cognitive task of understanding what is actually happening in front of their eyes and become the interpreters of reality."

Is this how we approach art?

Without analysing, criticising or re-appraising art, we indiscriminately accept it, as something mysterious, something beneficial, necessary and indispensable for the proletariat.

It is true that, at first, we argue a little, calling one thing bourgeois and another philistine. Subsequently, we seem to lack the most elementary knowledge and we immediately calm down as soon as a theatre, school, or an art workshop falls into communist hands.

It would seem as if this is all there is to it.

Surely, our activity has demonstrated the total inadequacy of such a solution to the problem.

What can we demand from our comrades, who are managers of some art department or some theatre, **when our so-called official ideologists insist on universal human values** and forget that "the social consciousness of all centuries, despite all the differences and all the variety, has so far revolved within well-known common forms, which will disappear completely only with the total destruction of the class struggle"?

They also forget that "the communist revolution is the most radical break with existing property relations; not surprisingly it also involves the most radical break with traditional ideas".

And they do not want to accept that:

The proletarian revolution is the first real step towards the communist transformation.

Destroying the bourgeois capitalist system, i.e. solving the question of power and transforming the relations of production cannot but overthrow the whole culture of the revolution's enemy.

Every day, the proletarian revolution shouts this out, but it is not accepted.

Every year, Narkompros [the People's Commissariat of Enlightenment] inflates like a soap bubble and bursts because its core gets excessively compressed by the spirits of all ages and nations, by all systems, and by all the "sinful" and "non-sinful" v a l u e s (!) of the living and the dead.

And under the protection of pseudo-Marxists, the "priests of art" in their black thousands work on, and, in our revolutionary times, the "spiritual" culture of the past still rests firmly on the crutches of reactionary idealism.

Artistic Culture, as one of the formal expressions of the "spiritual", has not separated itself from utopian and fanciful visions, and its creators do not renounce **the priestly functions of formalised hysteria.**

The communists of Narkompros, who manage artistic affairs, differ little from the non-communists outside Narkompros. They are just as captivated by the idea of the beautiful, as the latter are enthralled by notions of the divine.

Seduced by the priesthood, **communicators and popularisers** serve the past on their knees, **while promising the future with their words.** This impels them towards the most reactionary, déclassé, maniac artists in painting, sculpture and architecture. On the one hand, they are communists, ready to fall in open battle against capitalism at the slightest attempt at restoration; on the other hand, they are like conservatives, and are willing to fall without a fight, devotedly worshipping the art of those same cultures **that they judge so severely when recalling the theory of historical materialism.**

Unfortunately, our responsible and extremely authoritative leaders are not only dealing in a chaotic and unprincipled way with the art of yesterday, but also with that of today; and they are creating conditions in which it is impossible to set the problems of intellectual and material production onto the rails of practical activity in a collective and organised manner.

And this is not surprising, since they are of one flesh with those same pernicious aesthetes against whom the materialist-innovators of leftist art rebelled.

That is why a campaign is being waged both openly and covertly against "those without revolutionary ideas" and the "non-objective artists". And the richer the content of the latter, and the more obviously reality supports them —the less scrupulous the priests of the old art become in their struggle against them.

Officially, they are now supreme, they set the tone and, like skilful actors, present themselves as followers of Marx.

They are not followed by the proletariat, with its healthy Marxist materialism, but instead by millions of the masses; the intellectuals, agnostics, spiritualists, mystics, empirio-critics, empiricists, eclectics, and other chronic arthritics and paralytics.

It is these people who are now

defending artistic values

in the name of communism.

The priestly producers of these "artistic values" understand this situation and take it into account. They are weaving threads of lies and deception. Like the corrupt heritage of the past, they continue **to be parasites and ventriloquists,** using the resources of the same proletariat that, writhing in agony, is heroically implementing slogans **that promise to liberate humanity from all kinds of supernatural forces that are threatening its freedom.**

The hireling priest

is the person who can represent aesthetics and supply a series of palliative forms

for the intellectual and material culture of communism.

The proletariat and the proletarianised peasantry take absolutely no part in art.

The manner and the forms in which art was expressed and the "social" significance that it used to have did not affect them in any way.

The proletariat developed and cultivated itself independently as a class in the concrete circumstances of struggle. Its ideology was clearly and precisely formulated. It raised up the lower strata of its class, not through games, not through the artificial means of abstraction, not through abstruse fetishes, but through the real means of revolutionary action, concrete propaganda and agitation based on hard facts.

Art did not strengthen the fighting qualities of the revolutionary class of the proletariat, but rather corrupted several leading members. **On the whole, it was alien and useless to the class that had its own and only its own unique cultural perspectives.**

The more clearly the reactionary artistic wave of restoration manifests itself, the more sharply the healthy and authentic elements of the proletariat will dissociate themselves from this kind of activity.

During the entire period of the proletarian revolution, neither departments dealing with art affairs, nor organisations or groups have actually fulfilled their promises in action.

They have turned away from the widespread revolutionary slogans addressing the future to the reactionary bosom of the past, basing their activity on the theory of "spiritual" continuity.

Yet, practice has shown that "spiritual" continuity is hostile to the tasks of the proletarian revolution, through which we are advancing towards communism.

The counter-revolutionary activity of the bourgeois priests of art, who have irrationally approached the revolution from art, has created incredible confusion in its futile efforts to "revolutionise" the feeble spirit of the past by means of aesthetics.

The sentimental loyalty of the petty-bourgeois breed of ideologists to the revolution has created a deep split in the attempts to decapitate the materialism of revolutionary reality by using the old forms of art.

But the victory of materialism is on the eve of triumphing in the sphere of artistic work as well.

The proletarian revolution is not just a whipping word, but a real whip, expelling parasitism from actual human existence, whatever attire it uses to conceal its loathsome essence.

In the context of objective conditions, the present moment forces us to declare that the current state of social development is evolving under the banner of the unacceptability of the artistic culture of the past.

The fact that all so-called art is permeated with the most reactionary idealism is the result of extreme individualism, which impels it towards pointless new frolics with experiments to refine subjective beauty.

Art

is indissolubly linked:

to theology,

metaphysics

and mysticism.

It emerged in the epoch of primitive cultures, when technology existed in the "embryonic state of tools" and economic forms wallowed in extreme primitivism.

It passed through the forge of the craftsmen's guilds of the Middle Ages.

It was artificially kept warm by the hypocrisy of bourgeois culture and, finally, it crashed against the mechanical world of our age.

Death to art!

It naturally arose

naturally developed and

naturally came to disappear.

Marxists must work to elucidate its death scientifically and develop new forms of artistic work in the new historical environment of the present time.

In the concrete circumstances of our day, one can observe that masters of revolutionary art are inclining towards technological development and social thinking about their work.

Constructivism is advancing —the slender child of industrial culture.

For a long time, capitalism made it languish underground.

It was set free by the proletarian revolution.

A new chronology begins

with 25th October 1917.

On the far side of October are

The epochs of primitive,

authoritarian and

individualistic cultures

of power

and the spirit.

On our side

is the first culture

of organised work and the intellect!

Art depicted the cultures of the past, i.e. authoritarian and spiritual cultures.

"Beautiful" and "imperishable" art served religion, philosophy and all the so-called "spiritual" culture of the past, through its expressive means.

Art materialised "the spiritual" in a speculative way, illustrating sacred history, divine mysteries, cosmic enigmas, abstract sorrows and joys, the speculative truths of philosophy, and all the other childishness of adults, whose norms of behaviour were determined by the economic conditions of society at this or that historical period.

The social and political system, produced by the new economic structure, gives rise to new forms and means of expression.

Intellectual and material production

[redacted] will express

the emerging culture [redacted]

of work and intellect.

The first slogan of constructivism is down with speculative activity in artistic work!

We —announced the constructivists in their programme—

Declare uncompromising war on art.

Art is the product of the social life
of "crippled" generations.

Art is a product of social life.

Until now, its main social role has been to try to systematise feelings in artistic images.

This placed art in the category of social necessity, and it was automatically elevated to the highest level of cultural values, because it served a person's most subtle attributes, i.e. **feelings.**

The **"mystery"** of inspiration and the magic of **"destiny"** exalted this type of naïve human activity.

There have been people who have produced and venerated art at all times and at all levels of cultural and social development.

It [art] grew and developed in two directions.

On the one hand, it aesthetically assimilated (experienced) the prevailing psychology and ideology, preserving them in the static images of artistic expression; on the other, it worked on its formal substance and material means of expression.

The organisational functions of art and aesthetic experience possessed their own legitimate existence.

Ignorance and parasitical proclivities provided fertile soil for aesthetics of all kinds and qualities to appear as one of the means of cementing human society.

This was also helped by the fact that a person living according to "the laws of development of the external world" thought that these laws blindly forged their way in "the form of external necessity, in an infinite series of apparently random events" (Engels).

Moreover, a contemplative attitude to life also permeated the psyche, inclining it towards abstraction, self-deception, or self-indulgence.

As well as consolidating social moods and feelings in this way, art also fixed the life of society at one point, hindering the historical development of the social milieu, and creating significant obstacles in periods of revolutionary upheaval.

With the triumph of materialism and a conscious approach to the practical life of the active working masses —the organisational capabilities of aesthetics have proved to be inadequate.

"Eternal" and "imperishable" truths are now magnificently beginning to rot, decompose and contaminate.

And it is only the formal aspect of the business, the accumulated expertise, skills and other means of producing art that remain as a valuable heritage, which is used by the healthy circle of the revolutionaries of intellectual and material production.

We have arrived at these conclusions on the basis of what the Soviet Republic experienced when it tried to bring art into the service of the proletarian revolution.

To be more convincing for those who admire "scholarly historical digressions", we will summarise some passages from Professor Bogdanov's book.

For the moment, scientific data leads us to believe that the most ancient forms of art were dancing and music.

There are grounds for thinking that dancing and music existed even in the "zoological period of human existence".

When ideologies developed, "after the primitive age", art did not appear to be the source for the formal expression of these same ideologies.

It [art] served a purely practical function for primitive people and only possessed a utilitarian significance; it was an organisational element in work, creating a "unity of mood" among the participants and a connection between this mood and the work itself.

It is said that, even now, dancing and music play this role in the lives of tribes that still remain at the stage of a tribal or undeveloped way of life.

Using the available production technology for representing gestures, a savage wanting to communicate the idea of a certain object to someone else often unconsciously and spontaneously reproduced its shape through his movements.

This is considered to be the beginning of drawing and painting.

It stimulated an interest in and an aspiration to enhance observed resemblances.

In this way, humanity gradually arrived at the purposeful reproduction of the appearance of diverse objects

It was a means of acquiring knowledge about practical and important objects.

Tribes that hunted devoted their main themes and subjects to depicting animals and hunting.

The technical and economic character of this period did not develop beyond the limits of the embryonic conditions of tool production and the homogeneous and informal co-operation of related groups.

The primitive world view was not a well-organised set of systematic ideas. It possessed no ideological unity.

The processes of working and the facts of life linked ideas together, to a large extent, but they were still detached from one another.

According to the science of social consciousness, primitive dynamism and primitive collectivism are the basic features of its systematisation, which, with reservations, is self-generating "because the people of that epoch were incapable of doing it."

At that time, life itself was traditional, and the world view was not progressive. Although "work processes" were changing and becoming technically perfected, the designation of working actions still remained the same. They changed only slowly and gradually.

The forces for change lay in the area of technology, while ideology merely adapted itself to the transformations of working life that were taking place.

In conclusion the Professor states:

"Nevertheless, despite all its conservatism, ideology was a propitious and essential condition for progress."

During this patriarchal period, primitive farming and nomadic cattle breeding, as branches of production, supported the existence of an enormous communal economy. Authoritarian co-operation appeared with the expansion in the scope of co-operation, the emergence of specialisation, and the separation between organising work and executing it.

The technology and economics of labour entailed a large increase in the quantity of words, and the connection between idea and action was disrupted by life itself; the organiser's concept was implemented by the executor's action.

The mental effort of the leader, detached from physical processes, acquired independence, and ideas began to be systematised.

For the first time, there was talk about what we call a world view.

The idea of a cosmic organisation was taken from the only organisation with which people were familiar in their life, i.e. from the patriarchal community itself. Religion developed from the ancestor cult, i.e. from the veneration of ancestors, whom popular thinking gradually turned into gods, but in a quite everyday way, without the mysterious and mystical character that religion acquired later, when it detached itself from the rest of life, and became a special realm, encompassing people's entire world outlook and permeating all their thinking.

At that time, art was also completely religious: dancing and music were sacred images; myths, the unselfconscious poetry of the period, comprised the history of the gods and their relationships with people; works of painting and sculpture, even when they did not depict the gods, were "dedicated" to them and were successful, according to the beliefs of the time, only when they were inspired by the gods, which actually, they all were.

The transition from a patriarchal organisation of society to feudalism resulted from an increase in the productivity of labour, thanks to which surplus production increased to such an extent that it became possible for actual exploitation to emerge.

The forms of economic life in patriarchal society changed. Nomadic cattle breeding and primitive, semi-itinerant farming were replaced by settled farming combined with cattle-breeding.

The development of tool production led to the growth of handicrafts and such like.

The tribal community became a neighbourhood community. The organisers became differentiated: the civilians became priests, and the military, who were initially just leaders, subsequently became feudal "lords".

Already within the natural economy, exchange had become a permanent phenomenon, and had exerted a significant, stable and an ever increasing influence on economic life.

Gradually, extensive organisations —secular-feudal and spiritual-feudal— developed, which embraced entire regions and then large countries.

The religions of the feudal period represent a structure of the world, that was not modelled on the patriarchal community, but on feudal organisation. They became the basis for the priests' exploitation of the masses. The real world was supplemented by an imaginary world of demi-gods, gods, and higher gods, up to a single supreme god, forming exactly the same chain of authority as the ecclesiastical or secular feudal hierarchy.

Knowledge under feudalism gradually came to be divided into religious and secular.

In the same way, art was divided into religious and secular. Religious art predominated over secular. Architecture occupied the main position. Churches and other sacred buildings were unifying centres, which attracted the population of numerous feudally connected communities, sometimes of entire vast regions, sometimes of whole countries.

On religious feast days, thousands of people, who had no direct connection with each other in everyday economic life, gravitated towards the churches. There they were united in an emotional state of prayer, and then in the vicinity of the church, under the protection of its reconciling influence and the power of the clergy, they established more practical connections, exchanged goods, made acquaintances, concluded contracts, and so on. "Architecture*), just like its opposite, music, is a distinctive language of feelings. It expresses and gives a social form to human emotions, but also, of course, to the enduring, stable, and age-old passions of the masses. Whole generations, sometimes a whole series of generations, built enormous churches for the feudal religions, and the artists and constructors, being the children of their time, consciously, and perhaps even more unconsciously, expressed their dominant feelings and beliefs in their stone forms. The Gothic buildings of the Middle Ages, like Cologne Cathedral, are the clearest and simplest illustrations of the concept of architectural "style". Their slender, arrow-shaped lines, which soar upwards with enormous power, aspire, with idealism, profundity and vivacity, to renounce everything that is earthly and commonplace, striving towards the distant heavens. This is the fundamental sentiment of the Catholic religion, the consoler of the masses, which promised them heaven as a reward for the torments of this life, in which scarcity of land, the unbridled cruelty of wars, and the yoke of exploitation bore a remarkable resemblance to hell.

Architecture consolidated and conveyed the prevalent feelings of peoples and classes, without interruption, from generation to generation. Thus, the gigantic scale and massive forms of ancient Roman architecture were true expressions in stone of the pride of a people that had conquered the world. Similarly, when an aristocracy degenerates and becomes parasitical, architectural styles display an increasing and ever more bizarre complexity of forms, switching to subtleties and intricacies, frequently even to the detriment of the durability and practical suitability of the buildings created (the "baroque", and then the "rococo" styles). This expresses the pursuit of new, exquisite sensations, engendered by surfeit with its blunted perceptions, etc.

In the feudal period, architecture possessed a particularly profound educational importance. In the conservative environment of that time, it mainly acted as the keeper of the organisational tradition, by organising the emotions of the descendants, in conformity with what their ancestors had experienced.

Sculpture and painting in churches reinforced the role of architecture in the same way as the music of divine service did.

Secular art was far weaker than religious art.

Under feudalism, religious art was not only sacred, but also popular.

Emergent secular art was mainly connected with the needs of the secular, feudal overlords, in so far as they gradually came to represent exploitation, luxury and an enjoyment of life. This art had no roots in the masses, which was why it was comparatively weak.

Abstract fetishism in art appears in the individualistic society of capitalist production. The economy of such a society is characterised by informal co-operation, the exchange of goods, and private ownership of the means of production.

The fundamental features of art in an exchange economy are distinguished by the fact that art becomes the speciality of individual households and thus forms a number of distinct branches among others, working for the market, just as they do.

Works of art are regarded as the individual products of a particular master. There is no place here for anonymous folk creativity, which belongs to authoritarian cultures. In these, myths, fairy tales, epic poetry, songs, music and dances were not created by a specific individual, but by the community, the tribe, and the nation, just as architecture, sculpture, and paintings were: churches that were sometimes built by tens of generations under the supervision of unnamed architects, following one upon the other; sacred statues; icon painting in the churches, etc. In the ideal market society, such an anonymous and collective type of work is unthinkable, because it is based on a living link with society, which the artist-producer of goods cannot feel: he s e l l s his works, and experiences all the struggle and all the competition of the market.

---

*) From here onwards, the text is taken in full from *The Science of Social Consciousness.*

The social and organisational role of art eludes the consciousness of artists as well as that of society. Here, abstract fetishism is the same as in science: the idea of "pure" art and "pure" beauty is similar to that of "pure" knowledge, and "pure" truth.

The very subject matter of works of art is *individualistic*: they deal with the personality, in isolation and in relationship to others, its interests, its struggles, its fate, its feelings, etc. An individual, who feels mentally isolated, is explicitly or implicitly the hero of these works: explicitly, for example, in novels, poems, lyrics, and sculpture, where his experiences are directly portrayed; implicitly, for instance, in music and landscape, which do not portray him, but in their own way convey his spiritual moods, his aspirations and impulses.

Abstract fetishism does not consist of thoughts or images that are abstract, but is an abstract way of considering them, for example when a scientific truth or a work of art is regarded as something significant completely in isolation, unrelated to society, or to the life of which it is a part, i.e. as if its true meaning —its social function— were "abstracted" from it. In religious art, there was no such abstraction: the church or a statue of the deity was perceived as something that united the faithful to each other and to God himself, who was the idealised representative of past generations, i.e. art was a sort of social link. But supposing that the same statute of the deity, after several centuries, entered the market society, for instance, as an archaeological find; then it would be regarded more or less as a perfect image of beauty and nothing else. In actuality, however, it would still continue to link people who look at it in the same way, giving them some common knowledge concerning how powerful and harmonious life can be, and directing their feelings and thoughts towards unity. In short, it would continue to be a social link, albeit in a new form. But this function is hidden from the mentality of the market society.

The theory of "public art" is also not free from abstract fetishism, because it maintains that an artist must endeavour to make his works serve society, convey useful ideas, and inspire virtuous feelings.

This theory suggests that it is also possible for *art not to serve society*, i.e. it also does not acknowledge the true significance of art. Yet this significance —social and organisational— is always present in works of art. When society is divided into heterogeneous parts, a work may be able to perform this function well for some social elements, strata and classes, but poorly for others. Ostensibly aristocratic art is not suitable for democratic artisans, peasants, and petty traders, while democratic art will not suit aristocrats. Nevertheless, both have an organisational character, although they are directed at two different types of structure in society.

When art is required to offer itself consciously to serve, for instance, a political objective or a moral doctrine, it simply becomes an "applied" art of the kind that is used for the decoration and comfort of people's domestic dwellings.

For example, if art is political, it embodies an awareness of its link to a special political activity, but there is no understanding of its general organisational significance, apart from this particular connection. The theory of "public art" is just as fetishist as the theory of "pure art".

When we use scientific data, we are aware that the information which it supplies can be supplemented and changed. But for the moment, what it has achieved undoubtedly facilitates orientation, and helps us to perceive what is important: that art has never been something not made by human hands, something eternal, established once and for all. Its forms, its social significance, its means and its aims have changed in relation to changes in technical resources, economic, social and political systems, and the conditions determining the organisation of human society.

Concrete social phenomena are the products of practical human activity.

Concrete social phenomena are the products of practical human activity.

Hitherto, many people believed that “economic relationships developed by themselves, independently of us, and there was no need for us to interfere with them”. Now our intellect cannot be lulled into accepting such a definition. Otherwise, all the practical activity of the proletarian revolution would be completely nonsensical. Our contribution, however, resides in the fact, that we have consciously transferred “the forms of external necessity” and “the infinite series of apparent accidents” onto the paths of social purposefulness, without contravening the laws of basic logic.

Didn’t we manage to arrive at the Soviet system without infringing the laws of historical development? Didn’t this system, this new social structure emerge and develop under the conditions of a new economic structure?

It is developing, and the new ideology of this order is being formulated at present, although the balance of the economic system has not yet been achieved.

For a consistent Marxist, it is no surprise that new problems are also arising concerning the intellectual production of artistic work, which can only be resolved in all their concrete reality, practically, i.e. in practice.

“The materialistic doctrine”, says Marx, “that people are the products of circumstances and upbringing, and that therefore changed people are the products of changed circumstances and a different upbringing, forgets that it is people who change circumstances and that the person who brings up someone has also himself been brought up.”

It would be no sin to remember this now, and it would not hamper essential and serious work being undertaken openly in the area of the artistic work of intellectual and material production:

“A coincidence in a change in circumstances and human activity can only be correctly understood when it is conceived as revolutionary practice”.

Only in work, in practice, can the opponents of traditional art and the innovators of intellectual and material production prove the practical truth of their endeavour.

To gain for themselves this right, i.e. the right to concrete activity, and the possibility of production —this is the task of the present day, since the question “whether human thought can know objects as they exist in reality is not really a theoretical question, but a practical one.” (K. Marx)

“**Practical** activity must prove to a human being the truth of his thinking, i.e.

prove that he has actual power and has not come to a stop on this side of phenomena." (K. Marx)

"The main defect of materialism —including that of Feuerbach— was that it regarded reality, the objective world, perceived by the external senses, only in the form of an object or in the form of contemplation, and not in the form of concrete human activity or in the form of practical work.

"Therefore, the active aspect was developed by idealism, as opposed to materialism, but it developed abstractly, because idealism naturally does not recognise concrete activity as such." (K.Marx)

The art of the bourgeois capitalist era, being an external and formal expression of philosophical idealism in all its aspects, merely recorded the abstract, "active" side of reality itself, and in this respect its means of representation possessed meaning and a purposeful significance.

Painting, sculpture, the so-called noble art of architecture, and even the theatre —these are the material forms of the aesthetic aspect of bourgeois capitalist culture, with which the "spiritual" needs of the consumer of this unplanned social system were satisfied.

The proletarian revolution, having completely destroyed the artificial balance of bourgeois society, also exposed the stupid illusionism, absurdity, and acute contradictions of artistic activity. It removed the veils and lay bare the true face of sorcery, quackery, incantations, and rites —in a word, it struck at the very heart of aesthetic enchantment.

Many artistic values in their material formulation remained standing on the surface of the Earth, but the living, human material was shaken.

Being defines consciousness. Materialism entered concrete reality from the sphere of literary struggle, and entered in the most terrible way: it began to act practically.

Art, produced by handicraft, with its ancient technology, abstraction and abstract means of expression, stopped working.

Its place was taken by another, which was still timid, and had not yet found a precise or straightforward name.

Let us remember that each stage of social development must be understood in terms of those particular features that are unique to it alone.

At any given time, social phenomena are inter-connected.

"When dealing with social phenomena, one must proceed from the social and material forces of production, from social technology, and from the system of working tools".

"Would it have been possible", asks comrade Bukharin, "for the Eskimos of the ice fields to have invented the wireless telegraph? Or would modern science tell the future from the stars? Or could Marxism have emerged in the Middle Ages?

Of course not."

"The Eskimos of the ice fields would not have been able to invent the wireless telegraph because they were not even able to use a simple telephone. Modern science would not study such nonsense as fortune-telling from the stars, since the present stage of science rejects such things. Marxism could not have appeared in the Middle Ages because there was not even a proletariat. Marxism had no basis from which to grow.

"Now, take, for instance, advanced technology, the proletariat, the large number of newspapers, the gigantic scale of advertising, trusts, aeroplanes, the theory of electrons, Rockefeller's dividends, coal-miners' strikes, communist parties, the League of Nations, the Third International, electrification, armies of millions, Lloyd George, Lenin, etc. —these are clearly phenomena that belong to a particular period, a particular epoch.

"In exactly the same way, the phenomena of another period (the Middle Ages) were presumably the power of the Pope of Rome, relatively weak technology, the work of serfs in bondage to their lords, the science of clerics (scholasticism), the search for the philosopher's stone (with which it is possible to make gold out of base materials, etc.), the Inquisition, bad roads, illiteracy even among kings, the village community, witches, artisans' guilds, bad Latin (which was spoken and written by scholars), robberies by knights, etc.

Is it possible to transplant Lenin, Lloyd George, or Krupp to the Middle Ages? Is it possible today to witness a tournament with knights, fighting to the death for the sake of a lady's smile, on Red Square?

No. It's impossible.

Nevertheless, it seems that it is still possible to cast a shadow with art.

"With the help of all kinds of garnishes, we are offered Kings, Lears, Hamlets, Godunovs, Onegins and Tatianas and an infinite list of the names of dead heroes and villains of all times and nations —who are portrayed on canvas, cut out of wood, made up, dressed up, etc., etc.

And, at the same time, when nobody would think of using a horse and carriage as a means of travelling to Petrograd, we will calmly settle down, albeit metaphorically, into this or that era and study in a most serious way the hands of Rembrandt's old woman or the thighs of the Venus de Milo.

Enough of this idiocy.

Our culture is a culture of work and of the intellect, an age of advanced technology.

And just as the form of society is determined by the development of the forces of production, i.e. by the development of technology, so social phenomena arise, on the one hand, from the essence of a given form of society, and, on the other, from the means of technological achievements.

Our age is an industrial age,
and sculpture must give way
to the spatial resolution of an object.
Painting cannot compete with
light depictions, i.e. photography.
The theatre is absurd
when explosions of "mass action" are the
product of our time.
Architecture is powerless to stop
emergent **constructivism**.
Constructivism and mass action are
inseparably connected with the system of work
in our revolutionary everyday life.

It is essential to understand what the new ideology is in **reality**.

Infected by aesthetics, our Marxists not only honour the eternal truths of art and consider them absolute, attributing a sovereign significance to beauty, but they also regard art itself as sacrosanct and eternal.

In a fundamental way, this controverts the dialectical trend of the Marxist system and once again emphasises the unacceptability of opportunistic tendencies even when defining our attitudes to such subtle "matters" as beauty, aesthetics and art.

"When a chemist" writes Jules Destrée, "prepares a box of pills, and a shoemaker makes a pair of boots, the product of their labour has a quite specific and strictly limited purpose; what is produced will be used appropriately and worn out. In contrast, a work of art does not have this relative and limited nature.

It possesses an almost absolute inexhaustibility, and nobody is able to determine precisely the quantity of pleasant sensations, or the mass of sublime and benevolent emotions that it is able to evoke. Boots will be worn out, pills will take effect, but a work of art, after conveying spiritual pleasure to thousands of people, is still able to convey it to thousands and thousands more and in this way becomes an inexhaustible source of sublime joy for all mankind.

"Are any examples needed?

"Who is in position to enumerate all the noble and great thoughts inspired by the sculpture of the ancient Greeks?

"How much energy and courage does the sacred tune and poetry of "La Marseillaise" inspire in people advancing towards a better future?

"And these statues, these buildings, these melodies and poetry, which have produced so much hope, are always young and immortal, always inexhaustible, and always ready to provide the same sublime joys to all those who are able to admire them.

"These are sources of eternally fresh and infinite joys, treasured by all generations, one after the other, craving beauty"

It was necessary to introduce this long tirade from a representative of the opportunistic faction of socialists for the sake of saving time and in order not to quote the thousands upon thousands instances of verbal diarrhoea by our aesthetes turned "Marxists" or "Marxists" turned aesthetes, who in the same way shamelessly glorify "the superior demands of the spirit", "absolute inexhaustibility", "the impossibility of precisely determining the quantity of pleasant feelings", and "the mass of sublime and benevolent emotions" of "the spiritual pleasure" of "sublime joys"—in short, everything that is provided by eternal and imperishable art.

Indeed, are any examples really needed now to prove and enumerate "all the noble and great thoughts inspired by the sculpture of the ancient Greeks"? No, apparently not, they are not needed, simply, of course, because they are not necessary.

Living human activity is the best example and the most convincing proof.

And we think that "these statues, these buildings, these melodies and poetry", which are always young and immortal, and ready to provide the same sublime joy to all (admittedly) who can admire them —should be allowed to serve as an inexhaustible source of nourishment for all "crippled generations" forever.

And we, the rebels, must be more careful about feeding on the "nectar" of the immortal and eternal truths of beauty, as well as on eternal truths in general.

We know what Marx said about "the eternal truths" of the economic science founded by Proudhon.

He called it an illusion of "speculative philosophy".

It is a foolish trait in the intellect of a thinking Marxist to cling to these kinds of eternal truths, whose essence "is not destroyed by any subsequent developments".

If economic truths are merely the theoretical expressions of the specific historical relations of production, and as Engels states, with regard to sociological truths, "a limited relationship of connections exists only for given nations and for social and governmental forms, which are transitory by nature", then why must we allocate art such a permanent place in the panorama of intellectual reflection during this most dynamic stage of incessant social transformation, which is what the proletarian revolution essentially is?

"We must never forget that the knowledge that we acquire is necessarily limited by those circumstances under which we acquire it." In the same way, the emotions, about which ordinary aesthetes and our Marxist aesthetes boast, are also necessarily limited by the conditions under which they developed.

That is why "the demand for final solutions and eternal truths must lose all meaning, in our eyes, once and for all."

It is time to eliminate this foul atavism in ourselves.

If we know that the end of capitalist consumer society will also be the end of political economy, then we might ask, why should the end of an unplanned social economy, in which relationships between people were replaced by relationships between things, not also denote the end of a whole range of human functions, since fatalism, chaos and a lack of organisation will be replaced by planning and consciousness in the whole social life of the future triumphant communism.

But no more about this now.

In the present instance, it is important to determine when the change in art will finally be complete, whether the balance of class society has already been lost, and whether the social transformations are real and systematic rather than possessing a merely episodic character.

In order to pose this specific question with the utmost possible clarity, it is necessary to define concretely the contents of this particular change.

We are not concerned with that superficial change, about which there has been so much talk for four years.

The changes in literary themes and characters in the fine arts, decrees orientating subject matter towards the current political moment, and the promotion of formal archaism or social subjects from the time of utopian eclecticism —to call all this rubbish a revolutionary change and to present it as the new proletarian art is, of course, an absurd and therefore difficult undertaking.

It is shameful even to talk about this notorious "change", which is drenched in sentimental, petty-bourgeois spice and literariness.

For intellectually literate people, the subject-matter of art has never been its principal essence.

Although art, under duress, expressed the social ideas and emotions of the ruling classes through its subject matter, its foundations have always been rooted in its material and formal essence, in its production.

This production developed unevenly and slowly, only because like any form of production it was not free during the period of slave ownership, feudalism or capitalist bourgeois society.

Yet figurative art also did not serve the needs of society as a whole, like some sort of monolith.

Sometimes, it limited itself to the simple reproduction of manufacturing processes, or served this or that religious dogma or philosophical doctrine, or expressed the psychology of the non-productive class.

The ruling classes not only financially supported the material means of oppression, but also the intellectual forms, which helped to strengthen slavery.

And art, in its enslaved state, almost didn't manage to develop, i.e. to become differentiated in the substance of its form and production.

In its bondage, art was powerless to do anything but illustrate the "limited relationship of connections, which only existed for a specific time, for a specific people, and for social and governmental forms, which are essentially transitory by nature."

During the period of extreme eclecticism, i.e. during the period of bourgeois culture, in the depths of which the fresh forces of new historical stages were coming into existence, isolated innovators appeared from time to time, who had the courage to escape the snare of a "serf's" obligation to the ruling class.

Rejecting all "spirituality" and dogmatic ideology with a clearly expressed class bias, they stridently emphasised their production principles in solving formal problems in the fields of painting, volume and action.

Unable to find any practical role in a society that was officially in a state of decomposing, unable to assimilate the tasks of the new rising class, and becoming déclassé themselves through their own inner condition, artists confronted the dense walls of a narrow professionalism, divorced from life.

But proletarian October erupted.

Those who had supported and expressed the old were swept away.

This historical event, unique in its intelligibility, has highlighted precisely how the counter-revolutionary bacillus began to develop among the priests of art.

The aforementioned groups reacted completely differently to these events. Without assimilating the ideology of the working class, which had replaced the bourgeoisie, they, as producers, rushed into the maelstrom of general social reconstruction.

And we have not appeared at our best in fulfilling our communist duty in all fields of social production and reconstruction.

Old traditions, fetishism and atavistic pollution still held us firmly (and are perhaps still holding many even now) in the clutches of the hated past.

The petty-bourgeois pince-nez, which could not sit on our political nose, continued to fit tightly in the same place, when the scent of idealistic aestheticism was inhaled.

It is through this [pince-nez] that our responsible leaders have looked at the healthy foundations of the formal expressions of artistic work in intellectual and material production.

We did not have to wait long for the absence of any kind of clear line in the project of cultural construction, and of art in particular, to become apparent.

The admiration for experts definitively levelled the ground that had just been ploughed, and instead of assigning a fixed production plan to active specialist innovators, they [our leaders] flung open the doors to professionals in manufacturing spiritual images of stifling ventriloquism.

The change has not only not been realised in a positive sense, but it has also been received negatively and has frightened the people of Narkompros to such an extent that they have turned back to past centuries and to so-called classicism and academicism.

This is the change that we had in mind, when we asked about the legitimate date and month of its recognition.

But the Marxist aesthetes, foaming at the mouth, who vindicate the sovereign rights of eternal and imperishable art, are incapable of realising the fact that this horrifying and terrible change has occurred.

Citing the socialist foundations of Marxism, they claim that ideological superstructures and their formal expression are matters for the distant future.

Whether consciously or unconsciously, it's up to them, they forget or do not notice that just as the opinions of the creators of scientific socialism developed and became more profound over the course of several decades, so technology and the economic structure of society, along with the corresponding condition of the forces of production, have already changed to an adequate degree.

It is time to "admit" that the new ideology (of art), which is emerging organically from the new economic conditions, has arrived, despite all the obvious reluctance of the priests of aesthetics who hide behind Marx.

It is only necessary to understand what the new ideology is **in reality.**

How and in what forms it will now be implemented practically, under current conditions and in today's society.

From the speculative activity of art to socially meaningful artistic work.

Human *) society represents a system for unifying people. Above all, this association is a system of labour, an apparatus for human work.

The organisation and systematisation of ideas and the manufacture of goods take place without interruption within social production, under conditions of consistent interdependence.

The stone piles of cities, enormous buildings, railways, harbours, machines and houses —all of them are the material and technical "organs" of society.

Outside human society, any machine loses its significance as a machine: it simply turns into a piece of external nature, a combination of steel or wooden parts —nothing more.

Let us imagine that an ocean liner has sunk, that living bulk, with its powerful engine, which shakes the entire monstrous steel body of the floating house, and with its thousands of appliances of all kinds, from dish cloths to a radio transmitter.

When it is lying like a dead weight at the bottom of the sea, its entire complex construction loses social significance. The liner ceases to be a liner, because it no longer has a social life; it has dropped out of society, it has stopped being a part of it and it has stopped fulfilling its social role; from being a social object, it has turned into simply being an object, just like any other element of external nature, which does not come into direct contact with human society.

Technology —is not simply a piece of external nature; it is an extended organ of society, it is social technology.

In this way, objects acquire significance within "social life"; they enter human society as a technological system which forms its material working apparatus.

Man has extended his eyesight with field binoculars and the telescope. He has developed the telephone so that his hearing and voice will not encounter any so-called "natural" limitations and so that he will be able to speak and hear over hundreds of miles. He has pushed the capacities of his primitive means of transportation to their maximum potential and has literally begun to devour space by using engines.

He has even extended the wild frenzy of jumping to several thousand meters, the height attained by an aeroplane, taking off from the ground. All this represents the technical extension of man and his capacities.

*) The beginning of this chapter is written with reference to Bukharin (*The Theory of Historical Materialism*).

When we talk about social technology, however, we do not mean any one kind of tool or a group of different tools, but the system of these tools, and their sum total in the whole of society.

It is essential to understand that in a particular society, machine tools and engines, instruments and machinery, and simple and complex tools are dispersed in various places, but in a definite order.

In some places, they sit like large stacks (e.g. in the centres of heavy industry), elsewhere, other tools are spread around. But at any given moment, once people are joined together through the bond of work, and once we have a society, then the whole business is essentially interconnected, not only in our thinking but also objectively and in reality, and all working tools and all the so-called "technologies" of different branches of production form a unified whole, a single, social technology.

The technological system of society, the structure of its tools, also creates the structure of human relationships.

The economic structure of society is created by the sum total of its production relationships.

The social and political structure of society is directly determined by its economic structure.

But in periods of revolution, peculiar contradictions arise.

We are living in the world's first proletarian republic. The power of the workers is realising its pre-determined objectives, and is fighting not only to maintain power, but for supremacy itself, and to establish new and historically necessary forms of social life.

There is no room for speculative activity in the domains of work and intellect.

In the area of cultural construction what is really valuable is only what is inseparably linked to the general tasks of revolutionary reality.

Bourgeois encirclement can force us to make a whole series of strategic retreats in the field of economic norms and economic relationships, but it should not in any way pervert the process of our intellectual work.

The proletarian revolution has stimulated human thinking and deftly struck at the holy relics and idols of bourgeois spirituality. It has not only assailed the priests of religion, but it has also attacked the priests of aesthetics.

Art is finished! There is no room for it in the apparatus of human work.
Work, technology and organisation!

The re-evaluation of the functions of human activity, the link between each endeavour and the general scale of social objectives—

This is the ideology of our day.

And the more clearly the driving forces of social life challenge our consciousness, the more vividly its social and political forms take shape —the more the task confronting the masters of artistic work is:

To tear themselves away from speculative activity (art) and find the paths to concrete action, by applying their knowledge and skills to the service of actual, vital and purposeful work.

Intellectual and material production establishes working relationships and a productive connection with science and technology, replacing art, which by its nature cannot detach itself from religion and philosophy, and is powerless to escape the closed circle of abstract, speculative activity.

Tectonics

Faktura

Construction.

Preserving the stable, material and formal bases of art such as colour, line, surface, volume and gesture, materially meaningful artistic work will emerge under conditions of purposeful activity, and intellectual and material production will develop new means of artistic **expression**.

It should not reflect, portray, or interpret reality, but actually construct and express the planned objectives of the new, vigorous and active class, the proletariat, which is "building the foundation for the future society and building it as a class entity, as an organised force, which has a plan and great determination to fulfil that plan, whatever obstacles there may be!"

It is precisely now, when the proletarian revolution has conquered and its destructive and constructive process is laying down solid paths, which are advancing further and further towards an organised culture with a grandiose plan of social production, that people who can master colour and line, combine volumetric and spatial entities, and organise mass action must all become constructivists, in the common cause of construction and the movement of the millions of human masses.

In order to tackle this new work, which has never had a place before in humanity's entire working history, one must first of all discover fresh approaches to practical research.

To discover the communist expression of material structures, i.e. to establish a scientific approach to the business of constructing new buildings and services that will be able to meet the demands of communist culture in its transitional state, in its flux, in short, in all the forms of its historical progress, beginning with the period of destruction —this is the first task of intellectual and material production in the field of construction, i.e. of constructivism.

Its second task is to establish scientifically an approach to organising and consolidating mass labour processes and mass movements within social production as a whole, i.e. to develop the first planned scheme for the living "mass action" of humanity.

These are the fundamental and primary goals of intellectual and material production in the field of artistic work.

If we consider rationally the troubled reality through which we have been living since the first hour of the October days of 1917, if we analyse step by step the stages of the revolution's intensification, and grasp the complex manoeuvres of proletarian strategy, then we will realise how many misfortunes we have suffered and are still suffering because there were not and are not, always or everywhere, even a few trained comrades, able to perform consciously the jobs that are naturally emerging in the course of revolutionary development.

This phenomenon was apparent on all the fronts of the revolution.

We do not have in mind this or that specialisation or profession, nor this or that trade —that's not the point. Revolution is the highest form of social transformation; it demands specific knowledge and initiative, which are unique to it.

This practical truth could have been realised completely during the revolution itself, following the series of victories and the intensive efforts made to consolidate those conquests.

In art, too, something profound and significant happened.

Proletarian October provided fertile soil for the seeds of leftist art. Its best and most talented creators came to power. For four years, cadres, small in number but high in quality, were in charge of the country's art, re-organising schools and mobilising forces. But even in this happy atmosphere, they were not able to firmly establish new forms of artistic expression, because these leftist groups did not contain socially educated revolutionaries. They gave priority to individual and professional achievements in their fields of expertise over the tasks of the proletarian revolution. This was the main reason for their fall.

But the revolution is developing and becoming more profound, and with it the innovators of leftist art are also developing and becoming educated.

Intellectual and material production is confronting precisely this problem: with what means and how to create and educate teams of workers in the field of artistic work so that they will really be able to overcome and master those immediate tasks that literally spring up from the ground in front of us, at every straight line or bend in the revolution's path.

Formally, some of the masters of leftist art possess the exceptional talents and necessary skills to tackle this work. They lack an organisational foundation.

Constructivism is trying to achieve this.

It indissolubly fuses the ideological aspect with the formal aspect.

The masters of intellectual and material production in the sphere of artistic work are stepping collectively onto the path of communist education.

Scientific communism is the first and principal subject of their studies.

The Soviet system and its practice is constructivism's only school.

The theory of historical materialism, through which the constructivists are mastering history in general and capitalist society's fundamental laws and course of development, is also serving them as a method for studying the history of art. For a constructivist, the latter, like all social phenomena, is a product of human activity, conditioned by the technical and economic circumstances under which it emerged and developed. But, in the course of their general studies, the constructivists, who have a direct and immediate relationship to art as producers, are also creating a science of the history of art's formal development for the first time.

Bearing in mind that the present society is a society in transition from capitalism to communism and that constructivism cannot break away from its fundamental basis, i.e. from the economic life of this society, it considers the practice of the Soviet system to be its only school, where it is tirelessly and steadfastly conducting an endless series of experiments.

For constructivism, dialectical materialism is a compass, which indicates the paths and distant goals of the future. The method of dialectical materialism reveals an unexplored area, namely the design and development of new forms of material structures. This abstraction does not take constructivism away from empirical activity. The feet of constructivism confidently march upon the Earth, while all its ideas are found in communism.

In order to select from our own circle practitioners and theorists of constructivism, who are qualified in Marxism, it is essential to introduce a definite method into our work and to formulate disciplines [courses for art schools] that will develop and test all the constructivists' experimental working processes.

The leftist painters bequeathed a productive series of successful and unsuccessful experiments, discoveries and defeats. The second decade of the twentieth century had already witnessed their innovative efforts. Among these, rigorous analysis makes it possible to discern imprecise, but nevertheless persistent tendencies toward industrial principles: *faktura* [texture], as a form of presentation and as a form of painterly display for visual perception, and the search for structural laws, as a form of surface resolution. Leftist painting revolved around these two production principles, persistently fighting old traditions in art. Suprematists, non-figurative artists and "artists without ideals" came increasingly close to the pure mastery of the artistic work of intellectual and material production, but they did not manage to cut the umbilical cord that still tied them and connected them to the traditional art of the Old Believers.

Constructivism has played the role of midwife.

In addition to those material and formal production principles, i.e. *faktura* and the laws of structure, constructivism has provided a third principle and its first discipline, namely, tectonics.

We have already mentioned that the leftist painters, who developed under the conditions of bourgeois culture, refused to serve the tastes and needs of the bourgeoisie. In this respect, they were the first revolutionary nucleus in the sphere of cultural institutions and canons, and disrupted its vacuous wellbeing. Even then, they had begun to approach the problems of production in the field of artistic work. But those new social conditions did not yet exist which would enable them to think socially and express themselves objectively with the products of their skill.

The proletarian revolution achieved this.

During the four years of its victorious **advance**, the ideological, intellectual and contemplative representatives of leftist art have been absorbing the ideology of the revolutionary proletariat. A new ally joined their formal achievements

—the materialism of the working class. For them, the real professionals of artistic production, laboratory work on *faktura* and construction within the narrow confines of painting, sculpture and irrational architecture, unconnected with the social reconstruction of the entire social organism, has become as pointless as a mosquito bite.

And while the philistines and aesthetes, along with the chorus of the intelligentsia associated with them, were dreaming of how they could "harmonically deafen" the whole world with their musical art and tune its mercantile soul to the Soviet harmony;

how they could reveal the significance of the social revolution through their symbolist and realist pictures of illiterate and ignorant Russia, and put communism on the country's stages in professional theatres—

The healthy nucleus of the adherents of leftist art began to align itself with the revolutionary front itself.

From laboratory work, the constructivists have moved on to practical activity.

Tectonics

Faktura

and Construction

— These are the disciplines that will make it possible to escape from the dead end of traditional art's aestheticizing professionalism and set out on the path of purposefully realising the new tasks of artistic activity in the field of emerging communist culture.

Without art, the constructivist, through intellectual and material production, joins the ranks of the proletariat to fight the past and conquer the future.

Our Constructivism is fighting for
the intellectual and material production
of communist culture!

Before the proletarian revolution, each one of us, in our approach to work on spatial constructions, handled the material in an unsystematic way.

Assembling the material and the work itself were solved in detail, but did not possess a sound or well-established basis.

Everything was conceived in a narrow professional way and was artificially divorced from real life.

Inadvertently, work stopped and retreated into a game with experiments, projects that were known to be "outside of life".

It was essential to move on to real experiments within life itself.

Instead of creating abstract projects, our work must proceed from the concrete tasks with which emerging communist culture presents us.

Communism is essentially dynamic, and its first and most simple task is to realise a planned order and consciousness throughout the whole social and economic activity of the masses themselves.

Of course, having rejected and destroyed the old way of life, it will not allow the ugly forms of the old architecture to be preserved, or accept aestheticism. Its revolutionary activity in the field of the relations of production and production itself will place industry on new foundations, will pour technical energy into it, and only then will the "pearls" of the capitalist period be ruthlessly exposed, i.e. will be irrevocably condemned.

So whom will communism accept as its builder?

The architect who is an aesthete?

Certainly not.

The field of the spatial constructive building of the future culture will belong to the constructivists.

Before approaching the design of buildings, the constructivists must first work on themselves. They must set themselves the task of becoming qualified constructivists, and only then can they begin serious social work.

The transitional forms of social life and the material forms that express it often lack the most elementary outlines of constructivism, merely because actuality and reality do not encounter educated masters who can think dialectically and are able to give material shape to its fluctuations and their concrete essence.

Although it was necessary to immortalise something in the buildings of the past and place it on the Earth's surface in such a way that it would serve future generations as a silent symbol of eternity, once and for all, the constructivist's task embraces different practical considerations.

It is essential to teach ourselves how to build so that the dynamism of the product produced will not be an abstract or illusionary dynamism for visual impression, but an authentic dynamism of concrete movement.

What does that mean?

It means that if communism today needs a building for today, it must be provided, bearing in mind that tomorrow it will require the next form, and that this subsequent form must be supplied, so that it will not replace yesterday's form but supplement it, and in turn supplement the next form required.

Hence, for a constructivist to be able to build today, it is absolutely essential to know exactly what communism is and what it might require tomorrow.

So how should we approach this work?

Constructivists talk about "purposeful constructivity".

What is the essence of this constructive purposefulness and of purposeful constructivism?

It will only be possible to acquire a conscious mastery of the essential properties of constructive building by acquiring an absolute knowledge of the principles of communist economics and mastering the economics of the transitional period (from capitalism to communism), with a concentrated focus on the political and economic strategy of the revolutionary movement.

Purposefulness, therefore, must be understood as proceeding from the intrinsic qualities and requirements of communism, on the one hand, and from a conscious approach to industrial material, on the other.

Capital tried to organise bourgeois culture. It was the consumer. Art and technology fulfilled its requirements. Chance ruled in the competitive conditions of that way of life. The forms of the capitalist city, i.e. its architecture were also unplanned.

It is clear that the proletarian revolution, having radically changed social relationships, will also inexorably alter the forms of external expression. It is impossible and would be wrong to proceed from the conditions that are linked to the capitalist mode of living, with its fatalism, chaos and lack of will.

Purposefulness must be considered from the point of view of the present moment of the proletarian revolution.

For this, it is essential to study communism alongside specialist subjects, creatively understanding the initial forms of its emergence and the subsequent nature of its development.

The ideological part must go hand in hand with the formal aspect, i.e. they must be inseparable and mutually interdependent.

It is essential to actively participate in life.

There may have to be a long period of experimental activity for projects, but everything must be firmly established both formally and ideologically. Then the work will not flounder in a dead end of theoretical rationalisation. Undoubtedly, serious laboratory work will reveal numerous natural discoveries for the real requirements of communist culture.

The ideological part must direct practical concrete activity, while the experimental and practical aspect will undeniably correct and smooth out the ideological aspect.

Until now, people were building either monumental "works of art" or simply "properties for rent".

Apart from the fact that the word "monumentality" is rather hackneyed and commonplace —it cannot define the purpose of the new communist buildings. Its substance is steeped in values of taste and is governed by aesthetics.

"Properties for rent" were built in accordance with the principles of the market economy. They were decorated haphazardly, for commercial effect, according to the eclectic caprice of the private owner or the fancy of the builder himself, and speculatively clothed in a mixed style, but was most frequently modernistic. In America, these buildings were simply multiplied numerically, cutting vertically into space.

With tectonics as their first discipline, the constructivists are trying to eliminate the ignorance and arbitrariness of the architects and builders of the capitalist system.

Tectonics.

Tectonics or the tectonic style is organically smelted and forged from the qualities of communism itself, on the one hand, and from the purposeful use of industrial material, on the other. The word "tectonics" is taken from geology, where it is used to define the eruptions coming from the Earth's core.

Tectonics is a synonym for the organic, for the upsurge from the inner essence.

As a discipline, tectonics must lead the constructivist in practice towards synthesising the new content with the new form. He must be a person educated in Marxism, who has completely rejected art and really got to grips with industrial material. Tectonics is his lodestar, the reasoning behind his experimental and practical activity. Constructivism without tectonics is like a painting without colour.

Faktura.

It is not possible to approach a definition of *faktura* from the professional point of view of a painter. We must approach *faktura* materially, without investing the notion of *faktura* with

its previous meaning. We should provide a new definition for this concept and establish how *faktura* was understood before us and what *faktura* is in essence.

In analysing our concept of *faktura*, we should proceed from material in general.

As an example, we could take cast iron —an industrial material.

In order to make an article from it a complicated production process has to take place.

Cast iron is smelted, i.e. it is turned into a fiery liquid mass, then it is poured into a shaped mould, passes through the hammering section or is simply cut, and then enters the machine shop and the lathes, after which one can say that the cast iron has become an object. **This entire process is *faktura*, i.e. it is the processing of the material as a whole, and not just the treatment of its surface.**

Here, material is perceived in its raw state. The purposeful use of the material —meaning its selection and processing, and the nature of its processing for a specific purpose is *faktura*.

More precisely, *faktura* is the organic state of the processed material or the new condition of its organism.

***Faktura* as a word and a term has been used in different ways.**

***Faktura* signifies a recollection of the fact itself, the factual substance of this or another specific body or material.**

We are maintaining this meaning precisely.

Material is body, matter. The transformation of this raw material into some different state still reminds us of its original condition and communicates the possibility of its further transformation.

In so far as we transform and process material, we are involved in *faktura*. It follows from this that the second discipline can be formulated thus: *faktura* is material consciously selected and purposefully used, without impeding the movement of the construction or restricting its tectonics.

Construction.

Construction must be understood as the unifying function of constructivism.

While tectonics encompasses the fusion of the ideological and formal, and produces a unity of idea as a result, and *faktura* is the state of the material, construction reveals the process of structuring itself.

Thus, the third discipline is the discipline that gives form to the concept by using processed material.

Having developed these disciplines, the constructivists issue their second slogan:

"Long live the communist expression of material structures!"

The communist city is their steadfast aim.

As the mechanical and technical "organs" of society, our modern capitalist cities or cities of petty-bourgeois provincial comfort have turned out to be the staunch allies of counter revolution.

The experience of Soviet communism has demonstrated that the capitalist city not only does not accommodate even the most tentative signs of revolutionary re-construction, but what is more, it also obstructs the path of that reconstruction!

Its small and awkward buildings were cramped and have been unable to accommodate the operational requirements of Soviet organisations, just as the streets and squares have not provided the spatial conditions for mass actions and vast gatherings.

After all, both the external and inner substance of the bourgeois city, with all its eclecticism of architectural forms, is extremely subjective and tendentious.

The sign of private property protrudes at every step.

The disproportionate buildings, the unplanned scale of the streets, the decentralisation of the market itself, its dispersal into an endless series of small fragments, which exist independently —all of this makes it difficult to expose its logic, the structure of its technology and economy.

The whole city is decked in signs with extremely diverse inscriptions, in shop-windows, illustrations, advertisements, and numbers —but even this does not organise it.

Among the array of awkward, varied and bulky buildings, there are temples to the ruling religion, and the dominant art, monuments and other material attributes of a pernicious society, which infects the young with its spirituality.

It is essential to organise human consciousness and force groups of revolutionary activists and the working masses to see this ugliness as simply and naturally as they see the disorder in their homes produced by a change in their circumstances.

The communist city as developed in the constructivists' plans is the first step towards this.

Without communicating their fantasies about the communist city, the constructivists are now trying to take their projected plans out of the workshops and into the streets, in order to involve all the citizens of the proletarian republic in this great and communal venture.

Only in this way will it be possible to create a clear idea of communal property in citizens.

It is essential to get one's bearings in approaching a solution to the problem of "the communist expression of material structures".

Initially, as a first step towards the communist transformation, it is vital to take into consideration the experience of these past five years, during which the proletarian revolution has been reshaping the capitalist, bourgeois city.

Then, it should be observed how "NEP" [The New Economic Policy] is restoring it again, etc.

The constructivists are developing a systematic plan for all this work.

The first plan is a plan for determining: 1) What has to be done at the present time? **2**) Who can take part in this work? **3**) What forces and groups exist now? **4**) What has the revolution provided? **5**) What ventures have been realised? **6**) Information about cities in the present and the past. **7**) Building materials. **8**) A communist-orientated approach to reconstructing the city.

It is clear, when organising the work in the context of these factors, that constructivism's first practical measure will be directed towards purification.

We have to strip the bourgeois city bare. That is a very, very difficult undertaking.

For four years we have destroyed and demolished, but we have not managed to remove the bourgeois in an organised way and have not been able to approach what we urgently needed in matters of production.

The projected plan for the whole area of the urban territory, for individual districts, and finally the vertical spatial solution, the tectonics of the volumetric masses, the *faktura* of the material and the construction of its buildings —these are constructivism's main tasks, which arise from the fresh soil of the proletarian revolution, which is actively and consciously fighting for communism.

But constructivism also has other tasks.

To create a system for the design of objects in general.

The dualistic, i.e. twofold culture of the past divided everything into pure and applied.

Pure art and applied art, pure science and applied science, etc. It is possible with parallel vertical lines to construct an extremely long list of words according to the system of dualistic division.

The social roots of science, art and philosophy have never been mentioned, either because of the malice or the mental myopia of learned professors. Ideas seem to have been floating in the air, and the magic wand of divine inspiration similarly wafted in space over the sinful Earth, and from time to time descended on chosen men of science or art. But since the sinful people of this world did not sit with hands folded, but worked, this kind of dualistic split occurred.

"White devils" "made" the proletarian revolution. And strange as it might seem they did it so well that ideas flying in the air are no longer being hunted and the magic wand no longer risks touching the earth.

The end has arrived for the pure and applied!

It is now the time for the socially purposeful.

The working organisation of people is beginning the conscious production of intellectual and material culture. The social role of an object, from being solely of utilitarian significance, will be turned into a form of **general satisfaction.**

Technology forged from fragments of external nature, which consume enormous quantities of living human power for the organisational cohesion and con.

solidation of acts of production, will become the automatic and extended organ of society.

The material organisation of work, in part and as a whole, must not be effected simply, but constructed according to constructivism's unified plan.

Creating a system for the design of objects entails going through a long, practical process of conducting vital experiments, which are based on social purposefulness.

In addition, it is also essential to study the system from the formal and production aspect.

The constructivist Rodchenko, for instance, in explaining one of his experiments with spatial constructivism, writes:

"I have designed these latest spatial constructions as an experiment, expressly to link the constructor with the law of purposefulness of the forms used, the laws governing their combination —and also to demonstrate universality, to show how all sorts of constructions with different systems, sources and purposes can be constructed using identical forms.

"In the present works, as in real constructions, I have established an indispensable stipulation for the future constructor in industry:

"Nothing unplanned or unintentional", "Reduce everything to a universal initiative —simplify, generalise, etc."

Nothing unplanned or unintentional, nothing with irrational taste or aesthetic arbitrariness. Everything must be conceived in a technical and functional way.

Therefore, our constructivism, i.e. the constructivism that has developed on the territory of the RSFSR is strikingly different from the constructivism that is discussed in the West and with which our painters of leftist art are in contact.

Constructivism in the West.

The programmatic article of the first issue of the French journal *L'Esprit Nouveau* declared that "the new spirit is the spirit of construction" ("Il y a un esprit nouveau: c'est un esprit de construction"). The American magazine *La Vida Americana* announced in huge letters "the superiority of the constructive principle over the decorative".

Similarly, the Dutch journal *De Stijl* maintains that "the new collective style proceeds from the constructive principle."

[Ilya] Ehrenburg, the author of the book *And Still it Turns,* says about these declarations "Don't think that they are prophetic or visionary. These are simply sober conclusions based on real data. Artists have left the tower, looked at life and been astounded. There is a new way of life and a new man —inevitably there is also a new art."

To understand this change one must not study aesthetic manifestos, but seriously examine the context.

There were three stages before constructivism also emerged in the West as a new expression in the field of artistic work.

Before the War, during the War and finally after the Peace.

I. Before the War.

An abundance of things produced, but no perception of their value. Laziness and complacency. Immense successes in technology (aviation, submarines, cars, metallurgy, etc.). But only a few specialists understood them. The final echoes of the nineteenth century: theosophy, neo-Catholicism. Bergson, Claudel, Berdaiev, etc. The toad of individualism was puffed up to bursting point.

II. During the War.

Lies, evil, prayers and funeral services for salesmen, but not just that. The demonstration of organisation, although essentially hypocritical and hideous, was revealing in its external manifestations. The spectacle of the trenches, machine-guns, and weapons. **The rapprochement with the machine, the wonder of our age.** Impoverishment led to the clarification of work and things. The death of religion, despite shamanism and amulets. The camaraderie of the battalions, regiments, classes and peoples. The war was started in the name of hypocritical ideas, bigoted nationalism, romantic heroism, and a contempt for material things, but it ended with the triumph of internationalism, positive honesty and sober work.

III. After the Peace.

The convulsions of humanity trying to stand on its feet. Nationalists, competitors, philosophers, ministers and merchants continue the chaos of the past. But people, who understood the horrific experience of the war, have come to value above all: **Work, Clarity and Organisation.**

This trinity symbolises the creed of the new art. This is how comrade Ehrenburg, who left us two or three months ago, defines and explains constructivism in the West.

He took valuable material with him: photographs of our works, a notebook and a whole load of impressions.

The chief mistake of comrades Ehrenburg and Lissitzky is that they cannot tear themselves away from art

They simply call the new art constructivism. This allows them to group together the theatres of Tairov, Charlie Chaplin (Charlo), Meyerkhold, Mardzhanov, the comedians' flying expresses, circuses, Fernand Léger and many others, and call it all constructivism.

That does not mean, however, that constructivism as a phenomenon only belongs to us.

It is developing from all the conditions of existence, which are based on the state of the forces of production.

It takes different forms, therefore, depending on the condition of the forces of production, i.e. depending on different social structures.

The social and political structure of the RSFSR and that of capitalist Europe and America —are two entirely different structures.

Naturally, therefore, constructivism is not the same.

Our constructivism has declared uncompromising war on art, because the means and qualities of art are no longer capable of systematising the emotions of the revolutionary environment. The latter is consolidated by the real successes of the revolution, and its feelings are expressed by means of intellectual and material production.

In the West, constructivism is allied with art (the policy of compromise is a chronic Western disease).

Our constructivism has established clear objectives:

To establish the communist expression of material structures.

In the West, constructivism flirts with politics, claiming that the new art is outside politics, but it isn't apolitical either, is it?

Our constructivism is aggressive and uncompromising: it is fighting a harsh battle against chronic arthritics and paralytics, against painters of the left and the right, in short, against anyone who in the slightest degree defends the speculative aesthetic activity of art.

OUR CONSTRUCTIVISM IS FIGHTING FOR THE INTELLECTUAL AND MATERIAL PRODUCTION OF COMMUNIST CULTURE.

NOTES ON THE TRANSLATION

In producing this translation, I am greatly indebted to those scholars who have grappled with this text before me. In particular, I should like to acknowledge the extracts translated by Professor John E. Bowlt for his invaluable compilation of documents, *Russian Art of the Avant-Garde: Theory and Criticism 1902-1934* (New York: The Viking Press, 1976; and London: Thames and Hudson, 1988, pp. 217-225), and the complete version produced by Igor Serebriakov and published in *Russian Avant-Garde 1910-1930: The George Costakis Collection: Theory – Criticism* (Athens: Ministry of Culture, National Gallery and Alexandros Soutzos Museum; and Delphi: European Cultural Centre of Delphi, 1996) pp. 682-695. I should also like to express my gratitude to Lutz Becker, who gave me access to his own translation of Gan's text by Ben Barkow, Richard Davies of the Leeds Russian Archive for advice and also to Linda Aldwinckle, Maria Kokkori, Maria Mileeva, and Natalia Sidilina.

p. 8 This is a direct quotation from Karl Marx and Friedrich Engels, *Manifesto of the Communist Party* (1848; Moscow: Progress Publishers, 1952), p. 72. This translation was made by Samuel Moore in 1888 and edited by Friedrich Engels. Although it may read slightly oddly to English speakers today, it has the stamp of authenticity, which I thought it important to preserve.

Gan has used a slightly different spacing to that employed in the English translation of the manifesto. I have followed Gan's formatting of the text.

p. 9 "chronic incapacity". The word Gan uses is padagrizm, which is clearly a neologism that he created. It comes from podagra meaning gout. Gout is an infection that was traditionally associated with over-indulgence especially of alcohol and was often called the rich man's disease. One translation might simply be *podagrism* or *goutism*, but neither of these is particularly common in English and neither conveys the reactionary and self-indulgent qualities that the neologism implies in Russian. Since gout is a form of arthritis, I have chosen to translate Gan's term here with the explanatory phrase "chronic incapacity" and on p. 15, where it refers to people suffering from gout, as "chronic arthritics". These renditions do not have any class overtones, but are readily understandable.

p. 12 Karl Marx, *The Poverty of Philosophy: Answer to the Philosophy of Poverty by M. Proudhon* (Paris and Brussels, 1847); English translation, Karl Marx, *The Poverty of Philosophy* (Moscow: Institute of Marxism-Leninism, 1955; and Progress Publishers, 1955). In this criticism of Pierre-Joseph Proudhon, Marx formulated the distinction between utopian socialism and scientific socialism.

p. 13 Narkompros is the abbreviation for the People's Commissariat of Enlightenment (*Narodnyi komissariat prosveshcheniya*), which was set up in the Soviet Union following the October Revolution of 1917. Gan worked in both the Theatrical and Fine Art Departments of the Commissariat. Until 1921, these two departments tended to be manned by avant-garde figures, although other sections were run by more conventional personnel. As an employee of Narkompros, Gan was well acquainted with its structure and policies.

p. 15 The non-objectivists were the abstract artists who rejected a figurative content in their art. Non-objective or objectless art (*bezpredmentnoe iskusstvo*) is the term that Kazimir Malevich used to describe his Suprematist paintings, comprising coloured geometric forms on white grounds. Gan seems to have met Malevich and other avant-garde artists such as Aleksandr Rodchenko, Vavara Stepanova, and Vladimir Tatlin in 1918. As editor of the "Creative Work" section of the anarchist newspaper *Anarchy* (*Anarkhiya*) Gan actively promoted avant-garde art and ideas by publishing numerous statements by these artists. See the introduction for further details.

p. 28 Gan acknowledges in the text that he is quoting from Aleksandr Bogdanov. "The Science of Social Consciousness". The full reference is Aleksandr Bogdanov, *The Sciences of Social Consciousness: A Short Course of Ideological Science in Questions and Answers* (*Nauki ob obshchestvennom soznanii. Kratkii kurs ideologicheskoi nauki v voprosakh i otvetakh*, Moscow, 1914). It was republished several times over the revolutionary period. Gan may have known the text through his association with Proletkult or through his work as an ideological instructor for the Red Army.

Aleksandrovich Bogdanov (Malinovskii) (1873-1928) was a Marxist activist, scientist, science-fiction writer and theoretician He left the Bolsheviks in 1909, and after the revolution became involved in the proletarian culture movement (Proletkult).

Paragraph nine, beginning "The fundamental features of art…" is opened with inverted commas, although there are none following, so it is difficult to establish where the quote ends. I have chosen to omit these quotation marks since this whole section appears as an extended quotation from Bogdanov's *The Science of Social Consciousness.*

p. 34 Nikolai Ivanovich Bukharin (1888-1938) was a Marxist who held various positions in the Soviet government, including being a member of the Politburo (1924-1929) and the Central Committee (1917-1937), as well as editor in chief of *Pravda* (1918-1929). He also wrote numerous texts. He was a victim of one of Stalin's show trials in the late 1930s.

Ludwig Andreas von Feuerbach (1804-1872) was a German philosopher who advocated atheism, liberalism and materialism. His main book *The Essence of Christianity* (*Das Wesens des Christentums,* 1841) influenced Karl Marx and Friedrich Engels, but they subsequently attacked him for his inconsistent attitude towards materialism.

p. 35 The League of Nations was set up at the end of the First World War in order to prevent such conflicts in the future and to maintain peace throughout the world. It failed to stop the Second World War, and was replaced by the United Nations in 1945.

The Third International was also known as the Communist International or Comintern. It was set up in 1919 by the Bolsheviks in order to overthrow capitalism, foment revolution and establish communism throughout the world. It was dissolved in 1943.

David Lloyd George (1863-1945) was a member of the Liberal Party and the Prime Minister of Great Britain 1916-1922.

"the Inquisition", refers to various bodies within the Roman Catholic Church that were responsibly for persecuting all forms of heresy from the twelfth century until the end of the eighteenth century. The Inquisition was conducted with particular intensity and brutality after the Protestant Reformation in the sixteenth century and the ensuing Counter-Reformation.

"a tournament ... on Red Square", refers to Red Square in Moscow, which is in front of the Kremlin, the traditional seat of Russia's rulers before the capital moved to St Petersburg.

Krupp. The firm of Friedrich Krupp AG was one of the most powerful in Europe in the early twentieth century, and was successful in manufacturing steel and armaments.

"Kings". Gan is emphasising how inappropriate it is for theatre in the new workers' state, which has replaced the old Tsarist regime, to be putting on plays concerning royalty.

"Lears" and "Hamlets" Refer to William Shakespeare's characters.

"Godunovs". Gan is clearly referring to the opera composed by Modest Mussorgsky (1839-1881) entitled Boris Godunov, which he composed 1868-1873. The plot was based on the life of the Tsar of the same name, who ruled Russia during the time of troubles (1598-1605)

"Onegins and Tatyanas" refer to the opera *Eugene Onegin* (*Evgenii Onegin* in Russian) composed (1877-1878) by Pytor Tchaikovsky (1840-1893), which was based on Aleksandr Pushkin's (1799-1837) poem of the same name (written 1825-1832), in which a young Tatyana falls in love with Onegin, who spurns her love, and kills his best friend in a duel. Many years later he is smitten by Tatyana when he sees her at a ball. Mature, beautiful and married, she now spurns him.

"Rembrandt's old woman". Gan may be referring to the painting by the Dutch seventeenth-century painter Rembrandt Harmenszoon van Rijn, *Portrait of an Old Woman*, in the Hermitage Museum, St Petersburg. The painting was considered a paradigm of realism.

The Venus de Milo or *Aphrodite of Milos* was created in c. 130-100 BC, and is probably one of the most famous works of Greek classical sculpture. Found in 1820, it is now housed in the Louvre, Paris. Gan is obviously citing it as an example of classical art.

p. 39 Jules Destrée (1863-1936) was a Belgian lawyer, art historian, politician and a member of the socialist party. In 1894, he was elected to the Belgian House of Representatives as the deputy for Charleroi. His socialist ideas about art were elaborated in his book *Art and Socialism* (*Art et socialisme*, 1896). During the First World War he had visited Russia on a diplomatic mission. Between 1919 and 1921 he was Belgian Minister for Science and Arts.

La Marseillaise is the national anthem of France. Composed by Claude Joseph Rouget de Lisle in 1792, it was initially called the *Chant de guerre pour l'Armée du Rhin* (*War Song for the Army of the Rhine*). It acquired its current name because it was first sung in Paris by army volunteers from Marseille. In 1795, the French National Convention adopted it as the anthem of the Republic.

p. 40 Pierre-Joseph Proudhon (1809-1865) was a French politician, libertarian socialist, and was the first person to call himself an anarchist. He advocated Mutualism and workers' cooperatives. He first asserted "Property is Theft" in *What is Property? Or an Inquiry into the Principle of Right and Government* (1840). Friendship between Proudhon and Karl Marx ended with Proudhon's *The System of Economic Contradictions or The Philosophy of Poverty* which Marx attacked in *The Poverty of Philosophy.*

p. 42 "The petty-bourgeois pince-nez". Pince-nez were very popular in the decades before the Revolution in Russia, worn by figures such as the playwright Anton Chekhov. Gan may be referring (rather disparagingly) to Anatolii Lunacharskii, the Commissar for Enlightenment, who also wore a pince-nez and wrote rather traditional plays. Although Lunacharskii was generally tolerant and supportive of the avant-garde, he did not embrace their ideas wholeheartedly.

p. 47 Gan includes a note referring to Nikolai Bukharin's book *The Theory of Historical Materialism: A Popular Textbook of Marxist Sociology* (*Teoriya istoricheskogo materializma. Populyarnyi uchebnik marksistskoi sotsiologii*, Moscow 1922). The book explains how changes in the social and economic structure of society throughout history occur because of changes in the material foundation of society, i.e. advances in technology and modes of production influence how society and the economy are organised.

p. 51 *Faktura*. The Russian term *faktura* was based on the French word facture, which denoted pictorial texture or the way that the paint was applied to the canvas. It is usually translated into English as texture, but this does not adequately encompass its range of reference in Russia, where its meaning was expanded to embrace a variety of media and handling, even before Gan redefined it in the "Programme of the Working Group of Constructivists" and *Constructivism*. I have therefore chosen to retain the Russian term.

p. 53 "October days of 1917" refers to the Russian Revolution, when the Bolshevik Party, led by Lenin took over power on 25 October 1917 and subsequently consolidated that power.

p. 55 Suprematists. Suprematism was an non-objective, or abstract style of painting developed by Kazimir Malevich in spring 1915 and publicly launched in December 1915/ January 1916 at the *Last Futurist Exhibition of Paintings* "0.10" (*Zero-Ten*) in Petrograd.

The style, which comprised coloured geometric forms on white grounds attracted many adherents.

p.56 "laboratory work" is the phrase that the Programme of the Working Group of Constructivists (1921), written by Gan, used to describe works of art, which, as abstract experiments with colour, form or material, did not directly perform any utilitarian function, but could eventually help the Constructivists in the process of designing useful everyday objects for mass production and in the realisation of "the communist expression of material structures".

"Old Believers" belong to a Russian Orthodox sect, which was founded in the seventeenth century in reaction against reforms imposed on the church. They continue to cling to traditional liturgical practices and beliefs. For Gan, they epitomise extreme conservatism and rejection of all innovation.

p.63 "NEP" or the New Economic Policy was instituted by Lenin in March 1921. It was intended to resuscitate the economy after the devastation and disruption of the Civil War (1918-1920). It allowed small scale private enterprises to exist alongside state-run heavy industries. This compromise with capitalism permitted the re-emergence of entrepreneurial elements within Soviet society.

p. 65 This quotation is taken from Aleksandr Rodchenko's manuscript, entitled, "A Laboratory Passage through the art of painting and constructive spatial forms toward the industrial initiative of Constructivism" (*Laboratornoe prokhozhdenie cherez iskusstvo zhivopisi i konstruktivno-prostranstvennyie formy k industrial'noi initiative KONSTRUKTIVISMA*), 1917-1921 reprinted in Aleksandr Rodchenko, *Opyty dlya budushchego. Dnevniki. Stat'i. Pis'ma. Zapiski* (Moscow: Grant, 1996), pp. 109-115; English translation in *Aleksandr Rodchenko, Experiments for the Future: Diaries, Essays, Letters and Other Writings*, ed. Alexander N. Lavrentiev, trans. Jamey Gambrell (New York: Museum of Modern Art, 2005), pp. 123-130. The relevant section is on p. 125. The fact that Gan had access to Rodchenko's unpublished text reveals the depth of friendship between the two men at this point. Gan edited the text slightly, so that it reads a little differently from the artist's text as published previously in Russian and English.

p. 69 *L'Esprit Nouveau* (Paris, October 1920 – January 1925) was an avant-garde magazine edited by Le Corbusier and Amédée Ozenfant, which promoted modernist values through the publication of articles dealing with ideas in art, literature, architecture and science. In particular, it acted as a forum in which Le Corbusier could present his ideas on architecture and urban planning.

La Vida Americana (Barcelona, one issue 1919) was published by the Mexican artist Jose David Alfaro Siqueiros who was a communist and one of the founders of the Mexican Mural Movement.

De Stijl (Leiden, 1917-1920) was published by Theo van Doesburg. The journal promoted the theory of neo-plasticism as developed by Piet Mondrian according to which painting would express spiritual harmony and universal order by using only horizontal and vertical black lines, white and the primary colours of red, yellow and blue. *De Stijl* encouraged the extension of these ideas into sculpture, design and architecture.

Ilya Ehrenburg (Erenburg, 1889-1967) was a journalist and writer who had spent a considerable time in Paris before the Russian Revolution of 1917. In the early 1920s he moved to Berlin where he published his *And Still It Turns* (*A vse-taki ona vertitsya*, Berlin 1922), which promoted avant-garde ideas in connection with a new relationship between art and life.

Neo-Catholicism. Gan is using this term in relation to the general spiritual revival that occurred in the Roman Catholic Church during the XIXth and early XXth centuries. He is not referring to the movement as defined in 2002 in relation to the evolution of dogma.

The War refers to the First World War of 1914-1918.

Henri Bergson (Henri-Louis Bergson, 1859-1941) was a French philosopher whose ideas of duration, as a theory of time and of consciousness, exerted a strong influence on Russian intellectuals and artists in the early twentieth century.

Paul Claudel (1868-1955) was a French diplomat and writer, whose Symbolist poetry and verse dramas expressed his strong Christian beliefs and devout Roman Catholicism.

Nikolai Aleksandrovich Berdiaev (1874-1948) was a religious philosopher who was expelled from Russia in 1922. He was opposed to all constraints on creativity, emphasised spirituality, and was highly critical of communism.

El Lissitzky (1890-1941) was an artist who developed an abstract style of painting related to Kazimir Malevich's Suprematism of coloured geometrical forms against white grounds. In 1922, with Ehrenburg, he edited the journal *Object* (*Veshch'/Gegenstand/Objet*) in Berlin which promoted "constructive" art. This was based on a celebration of technology, science and the modern world. It embraced a vaguely radical social and political stance, and extended art into design, but unlike Constructivism retained a firm commitment to the work of art as such.

p. 70 Aleksandr Tairov (1885-1950) was an innovative theatre director, who ran the Chamber Theatre (*Kamernyi Teatr*) in Moscow He emphasised theatricality and the nature of spectacle in his productions, but he did not go as far as Vsevolod Meyerkhold in destroying the traditional relationship between stage and audience.

Vsevolod Meyerkhold (Karl Kasimir Theodor Meyerhold, 1874-1940) was an avant-garde theatre director, who rejected psychological realism. In 1922 he was responsible for the first Constructivist theatrical production, which combined a skeletal set that was like a machine for acting with a new style of acting that he called biomechanics, which fused the stylised gestures of *commedia dell'arte* with physical gymnastics and mechanised movements. This was far more radical than Tairov's approach.

Konstantin Mardzhanov (Konstantine Majanishvili, 1872-1933) was a Georgian theatre director who worked in Russia and favoured a stylised form of acting, returning to Georgia in 1922.

Fernand Léger (1881-1955) was a French painter who moved from Cubism to Purism, a style of painting that combined the precision of the machine with figuration and a populist subject matter.